ONE
ordinary
SUNDAY

"To say I loved this book would be an understatement. Paula Huston caught me up in her writing about the ordinary in Ordinary Time and sun-laced the quotidian again and again and again with that sense of *kairos*. What she has done is record in a single summer Sunday Mass what millions of Catholics have experienced many times over, using storied language that captures the sacred transfiguring the gray, foggy everyday of our ordinary lives. Her worries are our worries, her doubts our doubts, her convictions our convictions beautifully rendered and surprised by joy. I want to share what Huston has given us with as many people as I can. Bless her for writing this book and sharing an ordinary Sunday Mass which—like da Vinci's *The Last Supper*—manages to capture the divine amidst the turmoil and confusion of Christ's breaking of the bread on the night he was betrayed, when he gave himself, as he continues to give himself and as only God can."

Paul Mariani
Biographer, poet, and author of
Thirty Days: On Retreat with the Exercises of St. Ignatius

"Paula Huston has written an unusual form of autobiography: a story of her soul, narrated while she and her family are in attendance at an ordinary Sunday Mass."

Rev. Thomas Matus, O.S.B. Cam.
Author of *The Mystery of Romuald and the Five Brothers*

"Paula Huston does for us in the twenty-first century what Ambrose and Cyril did for Christians in the fourth. She wants us to know that an extraordinary thing happens at Mass on every ordinary Sunday. To her task of opening up the mysteries she brings a novelist's sense of drama and descriptive power as well as a convert's sense of discovery and wonder. She has made something beautiful for God and for us. This book will do much good."

Mike Aquilina
Author of *The Mass of the Early Christians*

"I loved this book. Avoiding the dull abstractions and overly philosophical notions of catechisms, Paula Huston educates the reader about the feel, history, and graces of the Mass and provides fascinating details about the purpose and meaning of its actions and symbols. *One Ordinary Sunday* will be illuminating not just for regular parishioners but for those who stand outside the Church and wonder what those Catholics are up to."

Ron Hansen
Author of *Mariette in Ecstasy*

ONE *ordinary* SUNDAY

A Meditation on the Mystery of the Mass

PAULA HUSTON

AVE MARIA PRESS AVE Notre Dame, Indiana

© 2016 by Paula Huston

All rights reserved. No part of this book may be used or reproduced in any manner whatsoever, except in the case of reprints in the context of reviews, without written permission from Ave Maria Press®, Inc., P.O. Box 428, Notre Dame, IN 46556.

Founded in 1865, Ave Maria Press is a ministry of the United States Province of Holy Cross.

www.avemariapress.com

Paperback: ISBN-13 978-1-59471-595-2

E-book: ISBN-13 978-1-59471-596-9

Cover image "Luce Splendente" © Fr. Arthur Poulin, www.fatherarthurpoulin.org.

Cover and text design by Katherine J. Ross

Printed and bound in the United States of America.

Library of Congress Cataloging-in-Publication Data
Names: Huston, Paula.
Title: One ordinary Sunday : a meditation on the mystery of the mass / Paula Huston.
Description: Notre Dame : Ave Maria Press, 2016. | Includes bibliographical references and index.
Identifiers: LCCN 2015037728 | ISBN 9781594715952 (pbk.) | ISBN 9781594715969 (e-book)
Subjects: LCSH: Mass--Celebration.
Classification: LCC BX2230.3 .H87 2016 | DDC 264/.02036--dc23
LC record available at http://lccn.loc.gov/2015037728

To Father Kenneth James Brown, with gratitude and love.

Contents

Preface

As usual, we are in the car and heading for Mass by seven o'clock in the morning. I love early Mass, and I love our parish church, and I honestly and truly love the little town in which we live, but on this particular morning, something seems a bit off. For one thing, I'm so used to having our grandkids with us—those bright-eyed children who lived with us for the past four years but have recently moved to another town—that this brand new day already seems drained of life. My husband, Mike, and I crunch down the gravel road beside the olive orchard to the aluminum gate at the front of our property, silently thinking our separate thoughts. I clamber out of the car, signaling our two Labrador retrievers to stay while I swing open the gate. Buddy, driven by puppyish enthusiasm, lunges for the dog cookie in my fingers, managing to give me a good, hard nip. And though I don't do it—I know better than to punch a puppy in the nose—for a moment I have to struggle with myself.

Though I haven't told a soul, for months I've been battling a vague gray something, a mixture of anger, self-pity, and secret sorrow. And everything that goes wrong—even Buddy's innocent transgression—confirms the general out-of-sync-ness of the world. I have a hard time falling asleep at night and an even harder time waking up. I eat too much or not enough. I understand there are reasons for this pall—within the past year and a half I have lost three key people in my life and my youngest sister has just been diagnosed with cancer—but whatever's eating at me these days is somehow bigger and more difficult to define than simple grief. I've burned through all my natural energy, and I can't quite get myself moving again.

I gaze out the window as we drive to church. The closer we get to the ocean, the thicker the fog. "June gloom," we call it, though in the past few years, it's been hanging on till nearly September. Yet I have to admit it: fog or not, we live in a beautiful place.

In Spanish, *Arroyo Grande*—the name of our village on the central coast of California—means either "large stream," "wide riverbed," or (according to longtime local wisdom) "big gulch," a designation that doesn't do justice to the rolling hills and twisted oaks and dramatic cliffs and white sand beaches that characterize this area. Originally populated by the Chumash, the valley was separated into two large Mexican ranchos in the 1840s, which were soon subdivided for settlement. By the early 1900s, Arroyo Grande's rich riverbed soil was already famous for its monumental output of fruits and vegetables. By the 1920s, Japanese farmers had turned it into a center for premier strawberry-growing besides. When newcomers arrived, they tended to stay.

Even nowadays, when tourism competes on equal footing with agriculture, we've managed to retain our rural flavor. We have vineyards—acres of them—and, increasingly, olive groves. We live in a semi-arid Mediterranean climate, which means we can grow almost anything here. People come to taste the wine and dip pieces of toothpick-pierced artisan bread into herb-infused oils. They come to pick olallieberries. And they come to walk the long beaches of the great bay that shelters us.

Maybe it's the ethnic make-up of this place—Portuguese, Filipino, Mexican, Italian, German, Irish, Japanese—that ensures the parking lots are always full at St. Patrick's, the one Catholic Church in town. The congregation gathers in a bland stucco building that in the seventies replaced the beloved but no-longer-insurable eighty-three-year-old edifice located on Branch Street. The St. Patrick's of today sits amid broccoli and cauliflower and celery fields across the road from the high school, and from my perspective, this is where the church belongs—in the middle of the farmland, among the crops, a mile or so from the windswept dunes and the great blue sea.

BECOMING A CATHOLIC

Neither Mike nor I grew up in the Catholic Church. His childhood spanned the forties and early fifties, mine the fifties and sixties, and in those days, religious affiliation was almost solely determined by ethnicity. I was a Minnesota Norwegian (and therefore a Lutheran), he was a Scot (and therefore a Presbyterian), and neither of us heard a good word about Catholics the entire time we were growing up.

The first time I attended Mass I was nearly forty. And like a lot of sixties' kids, for twenty years before that, I'd been away from church entirely. As a Lutheran, I was steeped in a liturgy very similar to that of the Catholics and part of a denomination that served communion in tiny individual cups every third Sunday in a ceremony that extended the normal worship service by twenty minutes. But this first-time Mass experience of mine wasn't anything like that comfortable observance of my youth.

I'd been invited by a Catholic friend during a period of extreme destabilization in my spiritual life. The atheism I'd espoused for the past two decades was suddenly up for grabs. God, or the "Hound of Heaven"—as a famous old poem calls this mysterious, urgent force—was clearly after me.

I'd like to say that it was the Mass that did the trick. That it was this introduction to the Catholic Eucharist, even watching from the sidelines and despite all the strange things I'd heard about Catholicism as a kid, that finally pushed me over the brink and back into faith. But that would be exaggerating. I was curious, impressed, even moved, but it would take a while longer before I succumbed to the stalking Hound.

However, I did not forget what I had seen that day. And I knew, despite my upbringing in a denomination founded by an erstwhile Catholic monk, that what I'd watched unfold during that Mass was qualitatively different from anything I'd experienced before. In spite of the similarities in word and gesture, it was clear that Catholics approached what I'd always thought of as mere symbolism with disconcerting reverence. The longer I dwelt on this first glimpse of the Mass, the more questions I had. Perhaps it was the seriousness with which Catholic communicants moved forward in their slow, quiet lines. Perhaps it was their gravity, so unusual in our day and age. Or perhaps it was that hushed mantra from the front of the church: The Body of Christ. The Blood of Christ.

What did Catholics know that I didn't know? What had I been missing?

I did not join the Church for several more years, but even before I officially signed up for RCIA (the Rite of Christian Initiation for Adults), I was hooked. I managed to slip into Mass nearly every day, hiding in the back row because I felt so out of place. Riveted by what I was seeing, I was not simply stirred in the intellectual sense but also magnetized both emotionally and spiritually. Whatever was afoot, I wanted to be part of it. Wanted this badly enough to set aside my sense of hurt shock when I was informed that, because of my divorce, I would first need to undergo a lengthy and cumbersome annulment process. Wanted it badly enough to wait the two years this would turn out to require. Wanted it enough to take on the distinctly uncomfortable task of telling my Protestant and more-than-a-little concerned family that I was becoming a . . . what? A Catholic? Really?

Even now, more than two decades after participating in my first Eucharist, I often find myself shaken when I partake of the Body and Blood of Christ. And as an "Extraordinary Minister of Holy Communion," as we lay helpers are called, I almost always gulp back tears as I distribute the Sacred Hosts or the Precious Blood. Yet as best as I can tell, these are not emotional tears, or even the sort of tears that spring to a person's eyes in the presence of great beauty. They seem to come from a place not normally accessible to me, a hidden place that only the Mass can touch.

One Ordinary Sunday began as an attempt to explain the mysterious power of the Mass in my own life. A personal meditation, so to speak. But I soon realized that an individual reflection on the subject could not possibly do it justice, for the Mass is a spectacularly communal event. As the novelist James Joyce so famously put it, when we are talking about the Mass, what we are really saying is "Here comes everybody." Even when a priest celebrates alone with a server, there is no such thing as a private Mass. As Pope Paul VI explains it, "From such a Mass comes a most ample supply of special graces for the salvation of the priest himself, as well as for all the faithful, the whole Church, and the entire world."[1] If I were to satisfy my own questions about the Mass, I'd need to address them on behalf of . . . well, everybody.

This includes Protestant siblings who have come to respect my Catholicism without knowing much about it, Jewish in-laws who seem unaware of the ancient Hebrew roots of Catholic practice, agnostic friends who have a sincere desire to understand more about religious faith, and formerly Catholic friends who've felt deeply wounded by their relationship with the Church. It includes people whose Catholicism is primarily cultural and people whose very sense of self comes from being Catholic. It includes new converts just entering RCIA and people who've been going to Mass since childhood. It includes people like myself who are periodically invaded by amorphous gray somethings as I am this Sunday morning. It even includes my friend Roger, famous for sitting in a back pew at Mass reading the *New York Times* and only rousing himself to go forward for Communion.

When I run through a list of all those who might possibly benefit from this book, the person who most quickly comes to mind is my friend Susie. A lifelong Catholic, she is steeped in a Church culture that sometimes still causes me to rear back in surprise. She made her First Communion at seven, was educated by nuns, got married in the Church, and raised her children in our parish. Now a grandmother, she faithfully goes to Mass every Sunday, tries her best to live virtuously and well, yet too often feels lost when she worships. And she's frank about her longing for more. As she puts it, "I might have been born into the Church, but I don't think I ever quite 'got' what goes on in the Eucharist. And now I'm at the place in life where I really want to know."

I am hoping that *One Ordinary Sunday* might help the lot of us, including Susie, see it all a little more clearly.

THE STORY AND THE SACRAMENT

The Mass is divided into two parts—the Liturgy of the Word and the Liturgy of the Eucharist—so this is the way I've structured the book. In the first section, titled "The Story," I sketch the biblical history leading up to the

Last Supper and Jesus' disturbing and seemingly incomprehensible command to "Eat my body and drink my blood"—a dictum his own disciples characterized as a "hard saying" and one that many of them could not, in the end, countenance. In the second section, "The Sacrament," I briefly examine the vision of reality held by the Jews and early Christians—Jesus' own world view—as a way to help recapture what our twenty-first-century eyes, trained to look upon the world through the lens of "scientism," can see with only the greatest difficulty.

Each of these sections is split into shorter chapters—for example, "Gathering," which discusses the opening processional, the Sign of the Cross and the priest's greeting; "Preparing," which talks about the Confiteor, the Kyrie, and the Gloria; and so on to the chapter titled "Going Forth." My hope is that by addressing the disparate elements of the Mass in separate sections, I can help illuminate, at least to a small degree, the beautiful and complex whole.

Though my research for this book has led me to the work of many wonderful writers, including Church Fathers, contemporary theologians, popes, and Church historians, my primary source has been the hefty, two-volume *The Mass of the Roman Rite: Its Origins and Development*. Written by the famous Jesuit liturgical scholar, Joseph A. Jungmann, it was first published in English in 1951 and led to Father Jungmann's serving as a liturgical expert at the Second Vatican Council. After months of poring over his incredible magnum opus, I have come to feel a real sense of connection with, and gratitude for, this remarkably erudite and unbelievably thorough scholar.

KAIROS TIME

By the time we arrive in the parking lot on this Fourteenth Sunday in Ordinary Time, I am already feeling a bit less morose. There's something about the sight of St. Patrick's, sitting amidst that lush produce, that can't help but lift a person. The squat, beige building topped by its simple cross with the usual starlings perched upon it reminds me of the many blessings of living where I do: our mild climate, our October-to-March rains, our creek-bottom soil, and the lines of dirt in the hands of our hardworking community.

Any moment now Mike and I will enter the sanctuary. And when we do, we will step back nearly two thousand years to once again experience what cannot possibly be experienced without the bridge through time we call the Mass. Yet this is not the half of it. For the Mass is a living liturgy, pulsing with the present, pregnant with the future. Each time we participate, we enter a different dimension that theologians call *kairos* time. This ancient Greek word refers to a suspended moment in which the chronological march of minutes suddenly seems to halt, allowing everything to happen at once. In this kairos moment of the Mass, we are healed and restored and spiritually fed. We are handed strong armor against evil. We are unified and made whole as a people and a Church. And we are ushered into a new kind of life—one that participates in the divine.

In other words, each time we come to Mass, we get a little taste of heaven. And this morning in particular, I am counting on that.

PART I

The Story

Introduction

Our grandson Eli, like any Old Testament character worth his salt, arrived amidst a whirlwind of panic and exhilaration. His mother Andrea had labored long and hard—twenty-seven hours—but in the end, his big head was too much for her. As I waited for my son-in-law Josh to tell me that the emergency C-section was over and everyone (please God, may it be so) was fine, I thought about Josh and Andrea's wedding three years before, the wedding of these fine young people who were now about to meet their big-headed first child, and what Josh had confided to me the night before the marriage ceremony. "I wish," he said, "that we could ride in on a goat cart while some bard chanted our family lineages."

"Really?" I said, momentarily stumped by the question of how we'd get our hands on a cart-trained goat at this late hour. "Why?"

"Because this marriage is not just about Andrea and me. It's also about everyone who came before us. I just feel that they should be acknowledged somehow."

He had a good point, I had to admit, and though we quickly got swept up in last-minute preparations and forgot all about the goat, much less the generational chant, it had come back to me when Andrea was still in early labor and they were trying to distract themselves by finally settling on a baby name. It was already a given that this child's moniker would honor at least one grandparent on each side of the family, though they both agreed that the appellations they chose should not be identical to but simply evocative of the names of their beloved elders. If it was a boy, they finally decided, he would be Eli Robert in honor of Josh's paternal grandfather, Edwin (an Eastern-European Jew who worked in the Manhattan garment industry), and Andrea's paternal grandfather, Bob (a German, Lutheran dairy farmer from Ohio).

Already then, little Eli, if that's who the baby would turn out to be, was firmly embedded in an ongoing, multi-generational family story. He would not arrive in this world as a self-contained being stuck with the task of creating a community for himself. He'd already been placed. He had kinfolk and a culture.

THE MASS AS FAMILY STORY

On the simplest level, the Mass is a reenactment of a similar, though considerably more involved, family story. Jesus, whose words of farewell to his beloved compatriots on the eve of his youthful death became the Eucharistic words of institution, did not come out of nowhere. He was a faithful Jew of the first century AD. People knew his parents. They knew the town in which he grew up. If there had been something like a modern high school back then, they would have known what sports he played, and, more importantly, how good he was. He was that familiar to them. So familiar, in fact, that a sizable number of his neighbors and close relatives could not imagine a bigger role for him than carpenter, and certainly not the identity of wandering teacher and healer that he seemed to be taking on once he turned thirty. Because he was so firmly placed within his own mostly rural culture, a milieu in which people worked long hours in the fields or on the water simply to put food on the table, many of them saw his public antics as presumptuous and possibly mad. Who did he think he was? Could anything good come from Nazareth? (See John 1:46.)

Yet their multi-generational family story had actually prepared them well for the arrival of someone like him. Faithful Jews, they'd been waiting for centuries for the long-prophesied one who would be mighty enough to defeat God's enemies and create permanent peace on earth. They were convinced they would recognize the great warrior king so clearly described in Psalm 21. They were sure they would know when the descendent of the legendary King David, destined to rule in perpetuity, finally appeared before them. True, these prophecies were ancient and fragmentary, difficult to comprehend, but together they formed a mosaic-like but compelling portrait—though not, after all, of a ruling dynasty but increasingly of a specific person: the Messiah, also known as the Christ.

The first half of the Mass, the Liturgy of the Word, takes us back to the very beginning of this family saga with an opening reading from the Old Testament (except for Easter Sunday and the seven weeks following when the First Reading is taken from the Acts of the Apostles). Within the pages of the Old Testament, we find ourselves in truly ancient territory. Most of the Old Testament did not take written form until about 2,500 years ago, but it draws on oral history that goes back to the dawn of time, opening with the great creation story of Genesis, during which God makes his first covenant with the human race. A *covenant* is not, as we might imagine today, simply a contract or legal arrangement that is invalidated when one of the parties violates it. It is a permanent alliance, a binding together, a new blood relationship. And it extends to everyone it represents, including succeeding generations.

Even though the biblical covenants (there are six of them) are permanent, not all of them are unconditional. They can result in both blessings and curses. Thus the Bible story is not conflict-free. Human beings created in the image of God, which means created with the capacity for real choice, regularly choose to go their own willful ways instead of honoring the terms of the covenants. Adam and Eve, for example, manage to violate in record time the simple requirements of this first basic agreement. Yet one of the great themes of the Bible is God's remarkable patience. Over and over again he offers his unfailing love and mercy to erring mankind. Over and over again he offers to bind himself in new and ever more complex ways to the human race.

Key to this family history is the arrival on the scene about four thousand years ago of a Sumerian nomad called Abram of Ur who, much to his amazement, is called by God to become the father of a "great nation," a people chosen out of all others to become a special sign for the world (Gn 12:2). According to the offered terms, if Abram agrees to leave his homeland and strike out for a new land that God will give him, God in turn will bless him with as many descendants as there are stars in the sky (Gn 15:5). And though it takes many years and Abram (now called Abraham) and his wife Sarah are far beyond the age of childbearing when it finally happens, God does indeed honor his covenantal promise with the birth of their first son, Isaac.

Five hundred years later, Abraham's many descendants—by now a vast tribe known as the Hebrews—are offered yet another binding agreement through their leader Moses, this time to anchor themselves in a moral and spiritual set of laws that will enable them to finally become God's sign of love and goodness in the world. In return he will lead them back to their lost homeland, protect them from the depredations of their enemies, and honor them with an important role in his unfolding plan for humankind. The first five books of the Old Testament, also known as the Pentateuch, comprise this Law or Torah, which is still the moral anchor for contemporary Jews.

In the Mass, the Old Testament reading is followed by a cantor-led recitation or singing of one of the psalms. The traditional Hebrew word for psalms is *tehillim*, meaning "songs of praise," though some of these are labelled *tefillot*, meaning "prayers," and a number of them are attributed to King David himself, an Abrahamic descendant who, thanks to yet another divine covenant, reigned in Jerusalem a thousand years before the birth of Jesus. There David's son, the famously wise King Solomon, built the first Temple. Some of the psalms were used in the earliest Temple liturgies, which means that psalm singing has been part of Jewish practice for nearly three millennia and part of Christian worship for two.[1]

Next in the Liturgy of the Word comes a reading from the Epistles, or the official letters of the apostles. Acting as both preachers and missionaries, the intrepid apostles Peter, Paul, Barnabas, Timothy, Thomas, and James spread the good news of Christ's sacrificial and redemptive intervention far and wide. They traveled to the modern-day Israel, Syria, Turkey, Greece, Italy and, by long tradition, Africa, India, and Ukraine before they died, often as martyrs. Almost invariably, the writer of the epistle for the day is Paul, the one disciple who never saw Jesus in the flesh but who became his greatest and most far-ranging apostle. Perhaps because of my own dramatic conversion experience, or perhaps because we share the same name, I have always felt a special kinship with Paul.

Finally, in this first half of the Mass, we hear from Jesus himself—the pivotal figure in this long line of descendants out of Abraham and the living sign of the last and most important covenant between God and man—during the Gospel reading of the day. Though the writers vary (Matthew, Mark, Luke, or John) the sermon, parable, or event is frequently connected in some deep and often riveting way with the Old Testament reading, the Psalm, and occasionally with the excerpt from an Epistle. Nothing in the Liturgy of the Word, in other words, is accidental. Nothing "just happens." Everything converges to a specific point in this unparalleled family saga, which Catholics believe is the Great Story, the Story of the Human Race.

Like all good stories, this one has a beginning, during which we find out what has precipitated this sometimes confusing jumble of events; a middle, in which characters collide and conflicts build but everyone keeps moving forward toward some as-yet-unknown conclusion; and an end, in which the conflict is finally resolved and we see the overall purpose of the story. The Bible does not, in other words, present a random universe. Neither does the Mass. They tell us that the earth and all that is in it was deliberately created out of nothingness by God. They tell us that he designed humankind in his own image and likeness. They tell us that throughout the course of history he singled out individual human beings—Adam, Noah, Abraham, Moses, David—for specific, important tasks and that because they were free beings, they were free to turn him down, which some of them promptly did.

But most important of all, they tell us that untold centuries after God's first ill-fated covenant with the human race, we still arrive in this world with the same inborn purpose as did those who have preceded us: to become participants in God's divine life. They tell us that we have a natural end to our time here on earth, a point toward which we are constantly, even if unconsciously, striving, even when it seems that all we are doing is failing. And when we choose that which leads us away from this natural end, we cannot help but suffer. Not because God turns on us and makes us pay for our rebelliousness, but

because we are in some deeply consequential way disre-
garding the person we are meant to be, the person we long
to be, the person God is so patiently waiting for.

THE LONG-ANTICIPATED INFANT ARRIVES

My son-in-law Josh was, if anything, more exhausted
than I was. Neither of us had slept, eaten much, or had
a moment to think during the hours of Andrea's difficult
labor. We had dark circles under our eyes. We smelled
bad. We no longer made sense. But when he tracked me
down in the empty labor room, he was ecstatic. "It's Eli!"
he said. "And he's fine!"

And soon the nurse brought him in, great-grandson of
Edwin, great-grandson of Bob, and now the newest member of our family. His head was a little large, true, but the
doctor assured us he would soon catch up to it. His eyes,
despite the long hours of birth trauma, were unbelievably bright. His birdlike mouth kept opening and closing
in what appeared to be utter bedazzlement. His mother,
despite her exhaustion, was nevertheless beaming with
grateful joy. He was here. He was fine. The long-awaited
infant had finally made his appearance.

Mother and child were installed in the bed, the lights
were dimmed, and the large cast of supporting characters—doctor, nurses, midwives—said goodnight and left.
It was time for me, the grandmother, to head for my hotel
room, find myself a large glass of celebratory red wine,
and crawl under the blankets for a long-overdue sleep.

What would they do, this new family, on their first night together? How would they handle it?

I should have guessed. Andrea tucked Eli into the crook of her arm. Josh lay down in the bed beside them. And then he held up a children's book—I can't, for the life of me, remember which one—and said, "Eli, my son, let me read you a story."

Gathering

The Opening Processional, the Sign of the Cross, the Greeting

As usual, we pull into the parking lot at St. Patrick's via the exit rather than the entrance lane, which is the best way to position ourselves near the actual exit, between Bill and Lynnette's modest SUV and Joe and Cindy's spotless white Acura. Every week after Mass, we head for Francisco's Country Kitchen or CJ's with these four good friends. Over eggs, fried potatoes, and homemade muffins, we mull over such hot topics as what's playing at the Fair Oaks Theater, when the next 20-percent-off sale at Miner's Ace Hardware is supposed to be, and how it is that Congress can't even pass a budget anymore.

Would we have met our breakfast buddies without St. Patrick's? Maybe. It's a small town, after all. But our bond is based on more than the fact that the six of us live in Arroyo Grande. First (with the notable exception of Mike, who is, ahem, older), we all graduated from high school around 1970. This means we are members of a generation that for the most part bailed out of "organized religion"

13

shortly after we got our driver's licenses. Second, we are Catholics in an era in which that's not exactly a social plus. To those outside the Church, Catholicism tends to be read as authoritarian, hierarchical, patriarchal, and puritanical at a time that values egalitarianism, feminism, inclusivity, and moral tolerance. The third and maybe most important reason for our bonding, however, is that we are part of the early morning "crew," meaning that most Sundays, most of us are fulfilling some kind of lay ministerial role during the Mass.

HELPING OUT AT THE MASS

Lay assistance of this nature is relatively new, at least in the last thousand years. Older Catholics can easily remember a time when the only people on the altar were priests and altar boys in lacy surplices. The Second Vatican Council, launched in the early 1960s by Pope John XXIII, changed all that. One of the key documents of the Council was *Lumen Gentium*, or "Light of the Nations," and in it Pope Paul VI, elected after the death of Pope John while the Council was still in progress, tackled an issue that had been simmering for a long, long time: namely, the question of what role the people should play in the Mass. Various attempts at involving the laity had been tried out by various popes and liturgists for centuries, but ultimately, the experiments had always led to the same conclusion: "For the Christian multitude," in the words of Joseph Jungmann, "the Mass should . . . remain wrapped under a veil of mystery."[1]

Yet before the chasm between laity and priests that began opening up in medieval times, things had been different for the people. And along the way, voices were raised, imploring the Church to reestablish that earlier and more intimate connection between lay folk and their worship. A good century before the Second Vatican Council, for example, Father Antonio Rosmini argued that "the people should be actors in the liturgy as well as hearers."[2] In 1897, the official prohibition on translating the Ordinary (the order, or established elements of the Mass) from Latin into the everyday language was quietly dropped by Pope Leo XIII.[3] And the movement toward increased lay participation continued to pick up momentum until Vatican II finally dealt definitively with the issue.

Which means that nowadays, it takes a lot of Catholics to celebrate the Mass. As we approach the narthex, I can see Bill, pharmacist by day and greeter by calling, occupying his usual position by the side door. Along with welcoming people to Mass, he and Joe serve as ushers, which means they collect the offering, then tally it up and stash it away in the safe. Making sure the money gets where it is supposed to go is a big responsibility in any diocesan institution—and our own diocese, which includes the four counties of Santa Cruz, San Benito, Monterey, and San Luis Obispo, is a large one, extending nearly two hundred miles along the coast.

Inside the main doors, Lynnette is standing with a short line of fellow greeters. A pharmacist too, Lynnette grew up on a dairy farm in what we Central Coasters refer to as "The Valley," and she and Bill often head there after breakfast at Francisco's to check up on her dad, the thoroughly Portuguese Manuel, who is now in his eighties and stubbornly, bowleggedly, still farming. I can see Pat and Larry, two of my fellow Lectors, bent over the Sunday Lectionary (the book of readings) studying their particular passages for the day. Larry, who by his own admission is beginning to deal with a few age-related challenges, prefers to be Lector #1, which means he will read the excerpt from the Old Testament. Pat, a former junior high school physical education teacher and incredibly in-shape grandmother of seven, will read from one of the Epistles. She will also read the Universal Prayer, or Prayer of the Faithful—public petitions on behalf of the global church, the world, the nation, and the local church, including the sick and those who have recently died—which is no doubt why Larry prefers the position he prefers; in our ethnically diverse church, surnames can be a bear, and he would rather screw up three-thousand-year-old Hebrew names than those of people he knows and loves.

Right beside Larry and Pat, the Extraordinary Ministers of Holy Communion, affectionately known in laid-back Arroyo Grande as the "EMs," are signing in and hanging their big wooden crosses around their necks. For the crowded 7:30 a.m. Mass at St. Patrick's, we usually need at least eight of these folks, who assist the priest during Communion by distributing the Body and Blood of Christ. Though under normal circumstances I love my EM job, today I am guiltily relieved not to be on the schedule. Extraordinary Ministers are supposed to be reverent, dignified, and, most of all, warm. We are supposed to look those who are receiving directly in the eye. We are supposed to project the love of Christ, no matter who might be staring back at us. And frankly, I'm not sure I'm up to that today.

In the midst of the milling crowd of EMs stands an already-robed Peter, recently voted altar-server-most-likely-to-be-bishop-someday. One of his many jobs this morning is to carry the heavy processional cross, a gold crucifix on a long pole that will be secured to a stand behind the altar. Something else I never saw during my Lutheran childhood—the corpus, or body of Christ, depicted hanging on the cross. Crucifixes came into wide use during the thirteenth century in response to the medieval focus on Christ's Passion. They are standard in Catholic churches today as a reminder of Christ's atoning act of sacrifice.

Beside Peter stands Rafael, a handsome young seminarian from St. John's Seminary in Camarillo who is doing his internship at St. Patrick's this summer. Like other would-be priests, Rafael is required to have an undergraduate degree, two years of additional philosophy, and four years at a major seminary before he can be ordained. Part of his training is to serve in a parish for a significant amount of time before ordination. Because Rafael is here to help Peter serve, there's no need for lovely, long-haired Brooke this morning. Another Vatican II-initiated change, rooted in *Lumen Gentium*: the role of altar server is no longer strictly limited to guys. Though there is still some controversy around that since altar serving has long been the gateway to the seminary, and in the Catholic Church women are obviously not eligible for ordination.

THE WOMAN QUESTION

Some of my non-Catholic friends are utterly appalled by this. How can you belong to a Church, they ask me, that so devalues women? Doesn't it drive you crazy?

I listen, wondering if they are talking about the same Church that has canonized hundreds of women and made four of them Doctors of the Church, "super saints" whose writing shapes official doctrine. I wonder if they are remembering the myriad nuns and sisters and abbesses and desert mothers who have acted as spiritual leaders through the centuries. I wonder if they've forgotten Mary. I'm guessing they probably don't realize how many roles women do fill in the Church: directing religious education programs, writing books, giving retreats, administering outreach programs to the hungry, serving as Lectors and Extraordinary Ministers, and acting as spiritual directors.

I clear my throat. Actually, I say, I would be incredibly disappointed should the Church ever decide to ordain women priests.

Stunned silence. My friends give me horrified looks.

I shrug apologetically. Look, I say. I grew up Protestant. The denomination in which I was raised was one of the first to ordain women. And I've known a number of wonderful women pastors—intelligent, dynamic, warm, highly educated. It's not a question of professional qualifications. Not even remotely.

Then what, my friends rightly demand, can it possibly be?

A couple of things, I tell them. Catholicism is totally rooted in the two thousand years of Judaism that gave birth to it. And Jewish religious practice originated in divine law and was overseen by a set-apart priestly male caste called the Levites. None of that changes in the New Testament even though Jesus had plenty of committed female followers he could easily have tapped for leadership roles if he wanted to. Yet though he makes it clear that men and women are spiritual equals, he chooses a man to take his place when he is gone. He says, "You are Peter, and upon this rock I will build my church, and the gates of the netherworld will not prevail against it" (Mt 16:18). And he then proceeds to bestow divine power on this man Peter by saying to him, "I will give you the keys to the kingdom of heaven. Whatever you bind on earth shall be bound in heaven; and whatever you loose on earth shall be loosed in heaven" (Mt 16:19).

Every Catholic bishop, I tell my increasingly dubious-looking friends, has become a bishop through the laying on of hands in a line of succession that goes back to the original apostles. The bishop's job is to impart the Holy Spirit to priests during ordination, which maintains this apostolic lineage. The Eastern Orthodox do it the same way. Both branches of the ancient church believe that not only would they be second-guessing Jesus' intentions if they were to start ordaining women, they also literally have no authority to do so.[4]

But for me, I add, the most compelling reason has to do with the Eucharist. This is the heart and soul of Catholic worship. Based on what Jesus said to Peter about the keys to the kingdom, Catholics believe that the presiding priest is acting *in persona Christi Capitis*, or "in the person of Christ the Head." Can you imagine how confusing it would be to see a woman in this role? Plus, it would rob one of our most important Biblical symbols of any meaning: Christ as Bridegroom, giving himself completely to the Church, his Bride.

Needless to say, my by-now overtly disgusted friends, sure that any impediment thrust in the way of an aspiring woman amounts to nothing less than retrograde patriarchal oppression, remain entirely unconvinced.

GETTING READY

By now, parishioners are flooding around us into the narthex, dipping their fingers into the holy water fonts, and crossing themselves. Both the holy water and the physical gesture (touching the forehead, the chest, the left shoulder, and the right shoulder while silently saying, "In the name of the Father, the Son, and the Holy Spirit") are meant to be reminders of Baptism. The water in the fonts at Catholic churches is often reserved from a store of water blessed at the Easter Vigil each year and used in the baptizing of catechumens, would-be members of the church who have just been through several years of RCIA (Rite of Christian Initiation of Adults) training, their long catechumenate a reminder of those early days of persecution when it was essential that people knew what they were getting into and why. As for that ubiquitous Catholic gesture, the Sign of the Cross, to cross oneself is to bless oneself. To cross oneself is to protect oneself. To cross oneself is also a great way to get one's head in gear for the Mass.

People are being greeted by Lynnette and her companions (handshakes, hugs, subdued affectionate squeals) and are heading for the pews. Some of them make full genuflections toward the tabernacle, which is the small, golden-doored, usually locked niche containing already blessed hosts. Centuries ago, the main reason for reserving consecrated bread in this way was for later distribution to the housebound sick, but as the *Catechism of the Catholic Church* explains, "As faith in the real presence of Christ in his Eucharist deepened, the Church became conscious of the meaning of silent adoration of the Lord present under the Eucharistic species" (*CCC*, 1379). Thus, the prominent location of the tabernacle—at St. Patrick's, on the wall to the left of the altar. People can come and sit before it, making their private devotions.

Along with being a visible sign of the central Catholic belief in the Real Presence of Christ in the Eucharist—the conviction that when Jesus said that his body was real food and his blood real drink, he was not kidding—the tabernacle is one of the most obvious reminders of the ancient family saga that undergirds Christianity. One of the first things Moses did after receiving the Ten Commandments from God on Mount Sinai was to order his wandering band of Hebrew exiles to build a special tent or tabernacle to cover the Ark that would permanently house the two stone tablets. This was a long and complicated project, but when it was finally finished and Moses had made his inspection, "the cloud covered the meeting tent, and the glory of the Lord filled the Dwelling" (Ex 40:34).

PRIESTLY VESTING

While Mike has a word with one of the Extraordinary Ministers, I poke my head into the sacristy, a little room off the narthex that serves as a kind of staging area, to see which priest is on duty. Father Ken, a good friend and former colleague of mine in the English department at the local university, has been lounging about on Maui and the Big Island for the past ten days, and I'm wondering if he's back and how it went and whether or not he ate any poi. This is new for him, this sort of solitary breakaway. He almost invariably takes his annual vacation to New Orleans, where his large extended family resides. "Hey," I say, spotting him rooting around in the closet. "Hey," he says back. "How's it goin'?" Though twenty years of teaching high-falutin' literature classes has ironed most of the Louisiana out of his voice, you can still hear echoes in the way he says "Hey."

He's already put on his alb, which is a long white robe that signifies purity and innocence, and he is in the middle of tying the cincture, the cord that belts the alb and rep-resents the virtues of chastity and continence. Based on the daunting symbolism of the alb alone, it's clearly not so easy to be a priest. The moral bar is extremely high and the fall from grace correspondingly steep, as we all learned to our great sorrow during the shocking abuse scandals that came to light during this past decade. Sometimes I wonder what it is like to be Father Ken, whether or not he ever wishes he were still grading midterms in a place where the only thing demanded of him was enough smarts to teach poetry to profoundly uninterested engineering majors.

We chat a little about the expensive (but worth it) luau Father Ken went to in Lahaina, and I leave him after he has draped his stole over his shoulders—the sign that he will shortly be engaged with an official priestly duty—and is positioning the green bat-winged, bell-shaped chasuble over his head. Chasuble colors change, depending on the season: green for Ordinary Time; white for Christmas, Easter, all feasts of Our Lord and Lady, and feasts of non-martyred saints; red for the Holy Spirit and martyrs; violet for Advent and Lent; white, violet, or black for Masses for the Dead and All Souls. Once in place, Father Ken's chasuble will fall in a graceful sweep nearly to the floor. And it represents (because every symbol in Catholic practice infers a major moral challenge of one kind or another) charity and the yoke of unselfish service to God. I leave because I know there are some private prayers he will be saying as he vests. Afterward he'll adjust his ear-bud mic, pat his pocket to make sure the sound is off, and gather up this morning's crew for a pre-Mass prayer. The Lectors, with Larry holding aloft the beautifully decorated Book of the Gospels, will position themselves side by side behind Peter, who despite his elfin stature will be manfully hoisting the heavy processional cross. Up front, Kathy-the-cantor will be holding her glorious and operatically trained voice in check (I always think of it as a sleek bay racehorse, dancing impatiently at the starting gate), while she waits for Father Ken's signal to begin.

THE MASS AS PLAY

Lots going on. And all of it, according to twentieth-century theologian Romano Guardini, who in varying ways was a wise mentor to our three most recent popes, in preparation for a kind of "play" that helps us attain internal order. As he describes it, "The liturgy has laid down the serious rules of the sacred game which the soul plays before God. . . . The soul must learn to abandon, at least in prayer, the restlessness of purposeful activity; it must learn to waste time for the sake of God, and to be prepared for the sacred game with sayings and thoughts and gestures, without always asking 'Why?' and 'Wherefore?'"[5] Pope Benedict XVI—writing as Cardinal Joseph Ratzinger—adds, "Children's play seems in many ways a kind of anticipation of life, a rehearsal for later life, without its burdens and gravity. On this analogy, the liturgy would be a reminder that we are all children, or should be children, in relation to that true life toward which we yearn to go."[6]

Mike and I head for our usual spot in the third pew. There we self-consciously prepare to genuflect (to kneel on one knee). Self-consciously, because this reverent gesture is one of those Catholic things we learned to think of as both medieval and weird when we were Protestant kids. What I personally like about genuflection and why I always do it, however, is because it is just strange enough in our individualistic, egalitarian era that it jars me into attention regarding the magnitude of what's about to begin. So we lower ourselves on our right knees until they touch the floor, making the Sign of the Cross as we do so, and then ease into our usual seats beside Candy, eighty-something Filipina and auntie extraordinaire. Both of us grasp her warm little hand and murmur early morning Mass kinds of things. She smiles and murmurs back.

THE PROCESSION, THE SIGN OF THE CROSS, AND THE GREETING

Then the pianist begins to play and Kathy's bay thoroughbred leaps through the starting gate with the opening bars of "America the Beautiful"—it's two days after the Fourth of July, after all—and the great procession begins. Father Ken's rich tenor rings out from the rear of the church. When they reach the front, the two Lectors will stand for a moment beside Father Ken and Peter. Larry will gingerly climb the two steps to the altar, the resplendent Book of the Gospels held high over his head, and he will place it in the special gilded book support, facing out toward the congregation. Peter will also climb the steps, securing the heavy processional cross in its stand behind the altar. Father Ken will go stand before the presider's chair, say without a trace of Louisiana in his voice, "In the name of the Father, the Son, and the Holy Spirit" as he makes the Sign of the Cross over his expectant congregation, and then he will offer us his official priestly greeting: "Grace to you and peace from God our Father and the Lord Jesus Christ."

Selfishly, I am glad not to be on duty this morning. Selfishly, I'm glad to simply be here. Sadly, that's what this lingering mood seems to be doing to me—making me selfish.

Preparing

The Confiteor, the Kyrie, the Gloria, the Collect

In the quiet space that follows, I think about genuflecting with Mike and how strange that still seems, even after all these years. Not only is it a miracle that either of us would ever choose to become Catholic, or—even less likely—that both of us would, but it is also a miracle that the Church herself would ever let us in. Why? Divorce is explicitly forbidden by Jesus, who said, "Therefore, what God has joined together, no human being must separate" (Mt 19:6). The *Catechism* adds, "The remarriage of persons divorced from a living, lawful spouse contravenes the plan and law of God as taught by Christ. They are not separated from the Church, but they cannot receive Eucharistic communion" (*CCC*, 1665). Thus, a would-be Catholic who has divorced and remarried automatically has a problem. And that was my situation when I began RCIA.

The priest explained that I might be able to obtain an annulment of my first marriage, which would be granted solely in regard to the circumstances of my life prior to that wedding. What the annulment Tribunal (Church court) considers is whether the former marriage was contracted freely and "without constraint." The process required that I submit a written autobiography, plus the name and address of my first husband and five other people who knew me well during my teenaged years (I married at nineteen). When I realized just how public this whole process was going to be, I was pretty sure I was going to curl up and die.

A year and a half later I was still going to Mass almost every day, still crossing my arms in front of my chest for a blessing instead of receiving Communion, and still waiting for a word from the Tribunal. That year and a half was at the same time one of the most humiliating and yet in some ways most enlightening of my life. Every day I passed in that limbo I was forced to think about who I had been back in my late teens and what I had ignored by way of good advice from people who loved me. But finally I got the word: in the eyes of the Tribunal, my decision-making ability had been constrained by "gross immaturity." Gross immaturity! I could not have been more thrilled. My annulment had been granted.

Though the Tribunal was right about my lack of maturity during that time of life—in fact, I managed to hold onto adolescence well into my thirties—I knew that in another way they were being kind. There was more to the picture, and that "more" took longer for me to acknowledge. Meanwhile, as I fell deeper and deeper in love with God and the Church, my list of questions grew. Who are we meant to be? Why do we cause each other so much pain? Why is there always this felt gap between our potential selves and who we actually are? My quest for answers led me into philosophy and theology and much reading of the Bible, particularly the gospels. What I found there should not have been such a surprise.

THE CONFITEOR

The diagnosis of our human problem offered by Christianity since its inception is remarkably straightforward and simple, despite being distinctly unpopular during these psychologically oriented times. And the explanation has not changed in two thousand years: the enormous moral and spiritual distress we so often suffer is caused by sin. We cannot, it seems, escape it; there is something in us that (to employ a carpentry metaphor) acts like a slightly askew wall measurement, leading to greater and greater distortion if we don't continually correct for the minor deviation from true.

One way we do this is through Confession. Though as Catholics we are convinced that "Jesus atoned for our faults and made satisfaction for our sins to the Father," that is clearly not the end of the story (*CCC*, 615). For no matter how hard we try to be good (and much of the time, let's be honest, we are not trying very hard at all), we keep running into the irrefutable evidence of our petty, judgmental, dishonest, unforgiving, greedy, lustful, miserly, lazy, vain, self-centered, self-indulgent, self-pitying, self-justifying self. Or at least I do. Which is why I find great relief in getting to a priest and laying it all out on the table.

But even after being absolved and vowing to be kinder, gentler, more loving, that askew part of us starts widening the gap once more between what we aspire to be and the person we too often are. And now here we are, a jumbled mix-up of good intentions and bad results, surrounded by the "here-comes-everybody" Mass crowd and wondering if we will ever get any better when suddenly we are halted in our tracks by the big hand of the *Confiteor*. The *Confiteor*, which is a confessional prayer that helps prepare us for reception of the Eucharist, is not a substitute for the Sacrament of Penance. It does not take the place of regular Confession, especially if we are involved in some kind of serious, ongoing sin. What it does do is get us in the right frame of mind. It creates in us a humble sense of our own inadequacy when it comes to our efforts at being good. It reminds us that we can't do it alone; we need grace.

And meekly we begin reciting in unison:

> I confess to almighty God
> and to you, my brothers and sisters,
> that I have greatly sinned,
> in my thoughts and in my words,
> in what I have done and what I have failed to do
> [here we give our chest three chagrined thumps]
> through my fault, through my fault,
> through my most grievous fault;
> therefore I ask blessed Mary ever-Virgin,
> all the Angels and Saints,

and you, my brothers and sisters,
to pray for me to the Lord our God.

THE KYRIE

I always feel better by the end. I am relieved at the words, "May almighty God have mercy on us, forgive us our sins, and bring us to everlasting life." I like the way Father Ken and all priests include themselves in this embarrassing self-revelation. And I especially love what happens next. Father Ken, in his fine tenor, begins to sing Greek phrases from the first three hundred years of Christian worship that did not make their way into the Roman rite until the seventh century and for whatever reason—perhaps because they were so beautiful in the form they were already in—were never translated into Latin:

> *Kyrie eleison* (Lord have mercy).
> *Christe eleison* (Christ have mercy).
> *Kyrie eleison* (Lord have mercy).

Each time Father Ken raises this haunting, minor-key cry, we repeat it after him, priest and congregation in an ancient call-and-response to the God who has reiterated from the beginning that he is indeed "slow to anger and rich in kindness" and that if we are interested in demonstrating our sense of grateful relief that he is indeed so, we can and should extend the same favor to those we'd rather condemn (Ex 34:6). "For it is love that I desire, not sacrifice," he reminds us in Hosea 6:6, and in case we are still not getting it, Jesus patiently explains what he means: "Be merciful, just as [also] your Father is merciful" (Lk 6:36).

THE GLORIA

The Kyrie, that mournful reminder of our recalcitrant human nature, is followed by the equally ancient Gloria. Neither come whole cloth from the Bible, though many parts of the Gloria are indeed passages from scripture. Both were written as early Church hymns, a genre that consciously mimicked biblical poetry and often modeled itself on the psalms.[1] Kathy and Father Ken are at their harmonic best during the Gloria, and as often happens during early Sunday Mass at St. Patrick's, I am momentarily awash in gratitude. Why? Perhaps because the Gloria is so joyfully sure of itself. In our supremely skeptical era in which it is intellectually much safer to doubt or—even better—to dismiss the very notion that surety is possible, the Gloria comes across like a happy parade of preschoolers banging their toy drums and tooting their tin whistles and tinkling away on their triangles, nobody caring two hoots about what any of it "means." That is the mood, anyway, and it is one I am especially grateful for today.

Given such insouciance, I'm always a bit startled at the actual words we are singing: "Glory to God in the highest, and on earth peace to people of good will." They sound like something angels would say, and in fact the first two lines paraphrase the Nativity section in the Gospel of Luke after the Angel of the Lord has made his stupendous announcement concerning the birth of the long-awaited Messiah: "Suddenly there was a multitude of the heavenly host with the angel praising God and saying, 'Glory to God in the highest and on earth peace to those on whom his favor rests'" (Lk 2:14). But while I'm still mulling these words over, Kathy and Father Ken have led us into the second section of the Gloria, and I have to sing faster to catch up:

> We praise you,
> we bless you,
> we adore you,
> we glorify you,
> we give you thanks for your great glory,
> Lord God, heavenly King,
> O God, almighty Father.

The final section of the Gloria is purely Christological, and much of it echoes the Nicene Creed. The Creed purports to answer the great question that triggered the first three Ecumenical Councils of the ancient world, which was, who in the world was Jesus? A man with divine powers? A god disguised as a human? Some mysterious and hard-to-explain combination thereof?

> Lord Jesus Christ, Only Begotten Son,
> Lord God, Lamb of God, Son of the Father,
> you take away the sins of the world,
>   have mercy on us;
> you take away the sins of the world,
>   receive our prayer;
> you are seated at the right hand of the Father,
>   have mercy on us.
>
> For you alone are the Holy One,
> you alone are the Lord,
> you alone are the Most High,
> Jesus Christ,

with the Holy Spirit,
in the glory of God the Father.
Amen.

THE COLLECT

Kathy stops. The piano stops. Father Ken gazes out upon us. Then he says, "Let us pray," and goes quiet so that we can make our silent personal requests of God. Today I find myself praying one name, over and over again—Tina. My youngest sister is at the very least facing a lumpectomy, then many weeks of radiation therapy. And that is the best scenario. Bad ones would include evidence of cancer cell invasion, lymph node involvement, or tumors in other areas of the body, which would involve more extensive surgery plus chemotherapy. Tina is scared. So are the rest of my siblings. So am I. Please, I pray fervently, restore my little sister to full and complete health.

Then Father Ken, acting as he is in the person of Christ, "collects" all our private prayers—the well-thought-out prayers along with the inarticulate and confused ones, the angry and uncomprehending ones along with the simply sad ones—and presents them to God on our behalf. This prayer, called the *Collecta* in Latin, is nowadays simply known as the Collect (pronounced with the emphasis on the first syllable), and it varies slightly from Mass to Mass in spite of covering the same basic four points: a call upon God, a recollection of some important deed God has done for us in the past, a specific petition, and a request in the name of Jesus Christ that our request be granted. When Father Ken is finished with this succinct little prayer, an inheritance from the days of classical Roman rhetoric, we respond with *"Amen!"* which is Hebrew for "So be it!"[2]

A JUST-HATCHED BABY CHICK

We sit. I pat Mike on his recently replaced knee. My husband gives me a sideways glance and a calm smile, which is an expression of his that is particular to early Sunday Mass. No matter what else has gone on during the past week—and it could be anything from broken water pipes to inexplicably bad sleep to brooding on his own past sins—my husband always looks different to me on Sunday mornings. In church, he has the face of a man who has just awakened all over again to a new reality, one that features stained glass and glimmering candlelight and the angelic voices of Kathy and Father Ken. One that, Mass after Mass, includes the *Confiteor* and its message of confession and forgiveness. It's not as though he forgets about all this in between, but it so easily slips into the background under the pressure of the to-do list. I know. It happens to me too.

But seeing that just-hatched-baby-chick expression on his face week after week is empirical evidence to me that something profound and mysterious and transformative really is going on here. Something as miraculous as the fact of our being Catholics at all. And that is something I can hang onto, even during times like now, when it seems as though I am wandering purposelessly in a dark wood.

Remembering

The First Reading

The exuberant Gloria has put me in mind of King David dancing naked before the Ark. I first heard that Old Testament story when I was kid in Lutheran Sunday school, and I have to say I was shocked. Naked? Really? Our Sunday school teacher assured us that it was fine: David was young and fit and ecstatically in love with God, so cavorting in the nude before the holiest artifact in Israel was entirely appropriate (this, remember, was the sixties). But I was suspicious, and later I read the story in 2 Samuel 6 for myself. Apparently, King David had not been entirely naked after all, but wore a peculiar priestly garment called an *ephod*, a linen apron that ties behind the neck and around the waist. This nod to modesty was not enough to stave off the jealous wrath of his wife Micah, however, who accused him of "exposing himself to the view of the slave girls of his followers, as a commoner might do" (2 Sm 6:20). I concluded that dancing in nothing but an ephod was somewhat like gyrating around in a hospital gown.

MICHELANGELO'S DAVID

Decades after that Sunday school lesson, I found myself standing open-mouthed in front of Michelangelo's famous and this time for sure entirely nude statue of David in the Galleria dell'Accademia in Florence, surrounded by a gaggle of adolescents (our children), who were just as impressed with him as I'd always been. I'd been awarded a generous writer's grant that allowed us to fly our four teenagers plus my recently widowed mom to Europe. There, we rented an eight-passenger van, picked up our former Dutch exchange student, Steef, and set out on a six-week, nine-thousand-mile trek through the continent. Despite the fact that we were camping, Steef (not much of a camper) had been eager to come with us. And now we were in Italy.

The temperature outside the Galleria dell'Accademia was a blistering 105 degrees, and as bedraggled, sweaty campers, it was sheer joy to be inside the air-conditioned museum. For a while, we just stood around admiring *David*. Then Steef asked, "I know he is from the Bible, but why was he so famous?" and I understood that one of the reasons she'd come with us on this rather grueling adventure was that she didn't know much, if anything, of the Great Story. Raised in secular Holland, she was now eighteen, officially a young adult, and because she loved us, she was trying to figure out what it was we believed in—why we went to church when nobody in her world did anymore.

Like other young people her age, she was part of the first generation to be born into a culture that was rapidly forgetting its Christian roots, and though she sensed a growing spiritual vacuum around her, she had no idea what that meant or what might fill it. Many of my English students back home, through no fault of their own, were in the same boat. Not only were they condemned to cultural illiteracy—for it's impossible to understand the great art and literature and philosophical ideas of the Western world unless we understand their Judeo-Christian underpinnings—these young people were in a state of spiritual starvation. And I knew that Steef suffered from that, whether or not she understood the nature of what haunted her.

But here, thanks to *David*, was a little opening. For the next hour, she and I sat on a long bench against the wall in an adjoining gallery while I gave her the Old Testament backstory of this handsome marble fellow. She asked some questions along the way, though not many. She did not seem to have any prejudices concerning faith; she simply knew nothing about it; she was a true innocent. When I finally ran out of steam, we fell into silence. A woman I realized I'd been seeing out of the corner of my eye for the past hour got up from a nearby bench and came over to us. "I'm Jewish," she said, "and I was nervous about what you were going to say to her about the history of my people."

I gulped a little. "And?"

"You did all right. Thanks." And she shook my hand and walked off. For her part, Steef sighed, got to her feet, and headed back to the great hall to admire *David* some more.

PEOPLE OF THE BOOK

Christians are often sometimes referred to as People of the Book—the book, of course, being the Bible. What this means in a practical sense is that the source of our faith is not fluid but fixed. We believe that the historical events described in the Old and New Testaments actually took place—for example, the four-hundred-year enslavement of the Hebrews by the Egyptians; the reigns of Kings Saul, David, Solomon, and Herod; the building of the Temple in Jerusalem; the birth of a baby in Bethlehem called Jesus. We believe that the more mythological-sounding parts of the Bible—for instance, the Creation story in Genesis, Noah's ark, Jonah being swallowed by a whale—are not only accurate and helpful symbolic representations of our Christian worldview but are also very likely rooted in real events that took place in the mists of time and were told and retold through centuries of oral tradition. We believe that the gems recorded in the Wisdom literature of the Bible (Proverbs, Ecclesiastes, Sirach, Wisdom) are not simply the interesting opinions of the gurus of the day but are actually real truths we can live by. We believe that the prophets were not just loonies in animal skins but real messengers imparting real messages from a real God. And we believe that many of the historical events, mythological stories, psalms, and prophecies of the Old Testament point directly to and validate the stories and events found in the New.

However, just because the words of scripture that form the basis of our faith are fixed, they are not moribund or set in stone but vibrantly, unceasingly alive. A good example of the unpredictable liveliness of the Bible is the Decalogue, also known as the Ten Commandments, which ironically enough actually were set in stone. The first of these great commandments, "I am the Lord, your God. . . . You shall not have other gods before me" (Ex 20:2–3), was both a general law and an urgent imperative of immediate and particular significance for the Hebrews of fifteenth century BC as they approached the border of Canaan, their Promised Land. The practical meaning of this commandment for them was that they were not to adopt the deities of the pagan lands they were entering, no matter how much easier it might be to assimilate themselves into this militarily formidable foreign culture than attempt to conquer it. They were not to worship Ba'al or put up Ashera poles on mountain tops or sacrifice their children in the ovens of Moloch. They were not to base their religious practice on what seemed most expedient or practical but were instead to present themselves as living exemplars of this radical new way of thinking.

CONTEMPORARY IDOLS

In the many centuries since, Ba'al, Asheroth, and Moloch may have vanished from the scene, but the injunction against idolatry found in the first commandment not only remains relevant but has in some ways become increasingly urgent. Our competing deities—those people and things and ideas that command our loyalty, determine our course in life, and fascinate us with their promise of an ideal world—do not take the form of golden calves or temple statues or mountaintop poles anymore but instead tend to be conceptual. What idols do we vest with the authority of God? At the very least, we bow down to the gods of psychology, political ideology, individualism, economic competition, and materialism (the pervasive belief of our time that only the physical exists). We see the world through the lenses they provide. We become the kind of people they require us to be. We play by their rules. And thus the First Commandment, originally imparted to Moses around 3,500 years ago, remains more relevant and more vibrantly alive than ever.[1]

Thus, if we think of the readings of the Mass as simply quaint accounts of times past, we miss the whole point. As Joseph Jungmann puts it, "[These readings] must be regarded entirely in the perspective of the present, for they are themselves bearers of the grace-laden message which God gives to men through his Church. The word of God in Holy Writ sounds with renewed vigor, waking in the congregation the consciousness of the foundation on which it is built, the spiritual world in which it lives and the home to which its path is directed. It is a message for this very hour."[2]

THE FIRST READING

After a moment of silence, Larry gets to his feet and heads for the ambo (the podium from which all scripture is read). He pauses for a moment, gazing reflectively at the congregation gazing back at him. "A reading from the Prophet Zechariah," he announces.

Thus says the LORD:
Rejoice heartily, O daughter Zion,
    shout for joy, O daughter Jerusalem!
See, your king shall come to you;
    a just savior is he,
meek, and riding on an ass,
    on a colt, the foal of an ass.
He shall banish the chariot from Ephraim,
    and the horse from Jerusalem;
the warrior's bow shall be banished,
    and he shall proclaim peace to the nations.
His dominion shall be from sea to sea,
    and from the River to the ends of the earth.
(Zec 9:9–10)

I think about this. The prophet Zechariah lived in the sixth century BC, five hundred years before the birth of Christ. Yet Zechariah was clearly envisioning, in specific detail, the great Palm Sunday scene in which Jesus enters Jerusalem for the last time, riding on a "colt, the foal of an ass." Zechariah prophesied that not only is this humble-looking rider the long-awaited savior and king of the Jews—the Messiah—but that he will be oddly meek in the face of those who are determined to torture and kill him. One of the reasons I find the Great Story so compelling is sitting right here in these few verses from Zechariah: There are no throwaway lines in the Bible. Everything connects. The past flows into the present, and the present predicts the future.

THE JEWISH CONNECTION

As a teacher, a parent, and a grandparent, I realize that I am becoming sad and worried about a loss of historical religious consciousness in our upcoming generations. Maybe, in fact, this worry is contributing to the vague uneasiness I've been carting around with me for so many months. Maybe I'm too aware that the now-ness of contemporary culture militates against kids picking up this ancient biblical wisdom about life, this critical knowledge about good and evil, in the old, natural way: through osmosis, watching their elders practice a faith that is by now thousands of years old and that provides our only real bridge to the past.

An observant Jew, Jesus may very well have heard this passage from Zechariah read aloud in his own synagogue, for the practice of reading passages of scripture at Mass comes straight out of Jewish tradition. In Jesus' day, two passages were usually read at each synagogue meeting, one from the Law (the Torah, or first five books of the Old Testament) and one from the Prophets. The readings from the Torah continued from one meeting to the next, so eventually the series began all over again. Later, after the destruction of Jerusalem and Herod's Temple in the year AD 70, this pattern began to change and by the time of the Talmud two hundred some years later, the Sabbath readings had been organized into one- or three-year cycles, depending on the particular practice of that area. However, even in Jesus' time, synagogue meetings included a *shema*, or statement of faith; a homily; a congregational prayer; and a blessing. The early Christian

Church adopted essentially the same pattern for its Liturgy of the Word.[3]

THE LECTIONARY

In Catholic churches today, the First Reading at Mass is taken from the Lectionary, a collection of selected passages from the Old and New Testaments. During most of the year, the readings come from the Old Testament, but during the Easter season, they are drawn from the Acts of the Apostles. In a similar fashion to Talmud-era Jewish synagogues, the Old Testament passages read on Sundays are arranged in three one-year cycles (cycle A, B, or C), and the particular passage for that day is chosen because it somehow relates to the scheduled Gospel reading.[4]

Thus, this prophetic passage from Zechariah that Larry has just read will be connected to the upcoming Gospel reading scheduled for this year's Fourteenth Sunday in Ordinary Time. One of the things I love most about the Mass is this carefully built-in coherence. Unlike daily life, in which I am periodically subject to mini-versions of my current case of the existential blahs, here in church, everything is woven together. The pieces fit. There is unity.

When he has finished, Larry pauses for a long moment, then says, "The Word of the Lord," and we, the congregation, respond with a phrase we find over and over again in the Letters of Saint Paul—an eminently grateful man, in spite of his many trials and tribulations. "Thanks be to God," we say, despite the reality of sin. Despite the array of contemporary idols that would lure us away from the narrow road of goodness and truth. Despite our growing cultural amnesia, which affects the Steefs of the world who've been spiritually deprived because of it.

"Thanks be to God," we say on this foggy summer morning on the Central Coast of California.

Responding

The Responsorial Psalm

During my own time of starvation, nearly twenty years into my away-from-faith phase, I was invited by a friend to go with her to New Camaldoli Hermitage in Big Sur, California, a Camaldolese Benedictine community of hermit monks founded in Italy in the year 1012 by Saint Romuald of Ravenna. I was taken there by the same friend who originally brought me to Mass at the Old Mission in San Luis Obispo, California, and when I first saw the monks in action, I'd already been slipping in and out of church for months, watching, thinking, debating with myself.

BENEDICTINE PSALM SINGING

One of the many things that struck me about life at the monastery was just how many hours a day are spent inside the chapel. The monks first appear in church at five thirty in the morning for a lengthy session of chanting, praying, and listening to passages of scripture and the words of an ancient Church Father. Most of this first service of the day, called Vigils, is devoted to the recitation of psalms in half-sung, half-spoken unison. Sometimes the monks, arranged in two facing rows, take turns singing antiphonally, with one side reciting the first verse and the other side reciting the next. Sometimes a cantor reads a whole psalm alone. That there is a strict pattern is clear; the selection of psalms changes with the changing days. The sixth-century Saint Benedict required his monks to recite all 150 psalms every week, and since the Camaldolese live by the *Rule* of Saint Benedict, they take this mandate seriously. This means that psalms are also sung at Lauds, which is the early morning prayer service that follows Vigils, sung again at Mass, and sung once again at Vespers, which at New Camaldoli is the service that closes the day.

Why are the psalms so important in monastic life? The Benedictine monk Paul Delatte puts it this way: "The psalter was created by God Himself to be forever the authentic formulary of prayer. With its thoughts and in its language God has willed to be praised and honored. The psalms express the deepest, most varied, and most delicate sentiments of the human heart, and answer all its needs. They served the saints of the Old Testament; they have served the Apostles and the saints of all ages. . . .They were said and said again by Our Lady and Our Lord."[1]

According to Delatte, Jesus, Mary, and Joseph no doubt chanted the Gradual Psalms (ancient psalms that were later used in the Mass) on their pilgrimages to Jerusalem. Some writers believe that Jesus' last words on the

Cross—"My God, my God, why have you forsaken me?" and "Into your hands I commend my spirit"—were simply a continuation of his daily praying of the psalms.

Though at first it felt odd and old-fashioned to spend so much time with the psalms, the more I participated in the monastic schedule, the more I came to appreciate these ancient songs of praise and longing. Not only do they articulate what is normally inarticulate—deep, private emotions like despair, self-pity, and secret anger, along with joy, delight, gratitude, and love—they constantly redirect my focus. It's impossible to remain self-absorbed when I am praying the psalms, which are always and ultimately about God.

THE RESPONSORIAL PSALM

After a brief silence, Kathy leaves her chair beside the piano and walks to the ambo to lead us through the next part of the liturgy, the Responsorial Psalm. The term *responsorial* actually means that the psalm selected on a given day "responds" in some way to the First Reading.[2] But it also refers to the fact that, as a cantor sings each verse of the psalm, the congregation responds with a one-line refrain. Kathy takes her place and the overhead screen lights up with the congregation's sung response: "I will praise your name for ever, my king and my God."

It's a funny thing about responsorial psalms: even though they are not meant to have what we usually think of as a "melody," a singable tune, but instead employ chant-like "psalm tones," I often find myself mentally humming the responses I hear at the 7:30 a.m. Sunday Mass. They get into my head—not just the arrangement of notes, but the words themselves. I think this is probably the point. For it is one thing to recite spoken words in unison and quite another to sing them with one voice.

The early Church seems to have understood this phenomenon well. For the first three hundred years, responsorial psalms were the vogue, with an individual cantor like Kathy singing the body of the psalm and the congregation offering its sung response. Because the refrain was repeated over and over, there was no need for a written text. You didn't have to be a trained singer to follow the simple melodic pattern. All you had to do was to listen and repeat.

Perhaps this explains why psalm singing goes back so many centuries—indeed, why it may well be one of the oldest aspects of the contemporary Mass. Some scholars have traced the practice back to the synagogues, where it was received as a legacy from Temple worship. If they are correct, then Saint Augustine's description of a psalm "which we heard sung and to which we responded" in the church of his day references a practice which already extended backward through 1,300 years of Jewish history. A famous contemporary of Augustine, the Greek Father Saint John Chrysostom was also clearly familiar with responsorial psalm singing, believing that the repeating of the refrain provided an entry point for deeper understanding of the entire work.[3]

Somewhat sadly, however, both men were describing a practice that even in their day was on its way out.

Following the legalization of Christianity in the Roman Empire in the year AD 313 via Constantine's Edict of Milan, churches had started becoming more magnificent and ornate, and the same held true for church music. Within Augustine's lifetime, greater emphasis would be put on artistry in the Mass, and soon trained choirs would begin to take over the role traditionally filled by the congregation itself.[4] And for many years to come—in fact, until partway through the twentieth century when the trend was finally reversed thanks to Vatican II—lay people would be given fewer and fewer opportunities for direct participation in the Mass. Nowadays, however, the responsorial psalm is back to stay, complete with graphics on an overhead screen.

Kathy launches into the refrain, singing it through once so we can get the simple melody. Then she lifts both hands, palms up, and we repeat it with her: "I will praise your name for ever, my king and my God." We are reciting what devout Jews in the days of Solomon's Temple would have called a *tehillah*, a "psalm of praise." Kathy sings each verse as we jump in with the repetitive response at each part in the text marked with an *R*.

> I will extol you, O my God and king,
>   and I will bless your name forever and ever.
> Every day will I bless you,
>   and I will praise your name forever and ever. R
>
> The LORD is gracious and merciful,
>   slow to anger and of great kindness.

> The LORD is good to all
>   and compassionate toward all his works. R
>
> Let all your works give you thanks, O LORD,
>   and let your faithful ones bless you.
> Let them discourse of the glory of your kingdom
>   and speak of your might. R
>
> The LORD is faithful in all his words
>   and holy in all his works.
> The LORD lifts up all who are falling
>   and raises up all who are bowed down. R
> (Ps 145:1–2, 8–9, 10–11, 13–14)

ADVICE FROM SAINT ROMUALD OF RAVENNA

The psalms are often the passages of scripture that speak most clearly and intimately to me. This, despite the fact that the context is usually foreign, the language archaic, and the sentiments of the praising or pleading psalms sometimes seem excessive by today's standards. I've come to believe that the power of the psalms lies partly in the individuality of their voices. Though many of them were certainly written by King David, others include ancient superscriptions—blocks of information that precede the song itself—that make reference to different names, though it is not always clear who is being referred to— composer or recipient. Still other songs (referred to as the "orphan" psalms) are anonymous.[5]

The best advice I've ever gotten in regard to the psalms comes from Saint Romuald of Ravenna, founder of the

Camaldolese Benedictines—the hermit monks of Big Sur who first introduced me to the practice of daily psalm reading: "The path you must follow is the Psalms—never leave it. If you have just come to the monastery, and in spite of your good will, you cannot accomplish what you want, then take every opportunity you can to sing the Psalms in your heart and to understand them with your mind. And if your mind wanders as you read, do not give up; hurry back and apply your mind to the words once more. Realize above all that you are in God's presence, and stand there with the attitude of one who stands before the emperor."[6]

As we follow Kathy through Psalm 145, I think about my morning and evening practice, learned from the monks, of reading, usually out loud, usually multiple times, the psalms for the day. I'm still amazed at how they absorb my full attention. Even in a communal situation, such as the Mass, they seem to have this power. For example, as I listen to Kathy sing, "The LORD is gracious and merciful, slow to anger and of great kindness," I am suddenly experiencing myself as I was forty-five years ago: a rebellious teenager with a hair-trigger temper and absolutely no understanding of the word *mercy*. It's an appalling flashback, and my first impulse is to block it. The refrain, however, relentlessly pulls me back into that awful teenaged self, and so I make myself stay there, knowing that if I do, the psalm itself will teach me something. As it does.

For then Kathy is singing "The LORD lifts up all who are falling and raises up all who are bowed down." Which in my case, he most definitely has. I am not that angry teen anymore—nor even that thirty-something in the midst of her extended adolescence—and haven't been for years. With this rare long view in front of me, thanks to the psalm, I can clearly see how I've been softened. I can see that by receiving mercy myself, not only from God but from my understanding spouse and all the other patient people in my life, I have gradually learned to curb my passions. Even to offer mercy myself.

THE PSALMS SPEAK OF MERCY

Augustine believed that all the psalms were in some way about Christ—either Christ as an individual human being or the Christ who abides in all of us as members of his Mystical Body. Christ, the bearer of mercy. Perhaps, I think, this is why I am so moved as I read them—or even better, hear them sung. For inherent even in the angriest of psalms is this vision of a mercy so vast and all-encompassing that it can never be conquered by evil. As such, mercy is the great expression of hope in a world that often seems hopelessly mired in sin. Saint John Paul II offers a simple but profound definition of this Christlike mercy in his encyclical *Dives in Misericordia*, "Mercy expresses our love for people without any discrimination, without difference of race, culture, language, or world outlook, without distinction between friends and enemies, desiring the true good for all."[7]

Pope Francis, who recently declared an Extraordinary Jubilee of Mercy, a whole year dedicated to the living out of this central biblical tenet, reminds us that "the Church is commissioned to announce the mercy of God, the beating heart of the Gospel, which in its own way must penetrate the heart and mind of every person. . . . Wherever the Church is present, the mercy of the Father must be evident. . . . Wherever there are Christians, everyone should find an oasis of mercy."[8]

In the ancient way of the church, now once again restored, I join in with my brothers and sisters as together we sing the refrain for the final time: "I will praise your name forever, my king and my God." And Kathy, from the ambo, beams down upon us, for we are doing surprisingly well indeed, despite the earliness of the hour, despite the grayness of the day.

Reconnecting

The Second Reading

That flashback to my angry teenage years has made me think about my mother, one of those beloved people in my life who died during this past year and a half. Poor Mom. Poor me. It was not an easy love for either of us. Whatever went wrong at the beginning of our relationship—my six months of screaming colic as a newborn did not help the situation, I am sure—my anger toward her was both self-righteous and implacable. Though we both survived those tumultuous teenaged years of mine, we could never quite get past the habit of walking on eggshells around each other. Even when I was fifty, Mom could still push my buttons.

Yet perhaps because we got our private moment of reconciliation at the end—a kiss of peace I will never forget—her presence lingers. This is partly because she made me her trustee—me!—when she had four other offspring to choose from, though even here her reasoning made me squirm: *You know why. It's because you're the only one who'll be able to pull the plug on me.* But she has also been present through the physical artifacts she left behind. Mike and I have a big barn, the only large and virtually empty storage space in the family, and so along with being the custodian of her financial records, I became by default the temporary caretaker of all her other important effects. Included among these were hundreds upon hundreds of hand-written, typed, carbon-copied, or e-mailed letters. And not just her letters, but pretty well all the family correspondence going back to about 1853 when my Norwegian great-great-grandfather first arrived in America.

My sister Tina, bless her, offered from the beginning to give them a permanent home. The only problem was that I live in California, and she lives in Ohio, and the cost of shipping all these boxes to her was prohibitive. So eighteen months after Mom's death, we hatched a plan. Mike and I would hitch up our fifth-wheel trailer, stuff it full of these priceless boxes of family heirlooms, and make our way across the Mojave Desert, over the Rockies, across Nebraska, to Minnesota where we would pick up my sister Gretchen as a third driver, then continue on our way east to Cleveland.

Meanwhile, I had to cut twenty-four heavy boxes down to a reasonable pile. Up until the night before the morning we left, I was still sorting through the epistolary remains of several generations. Maybe because I was doing it alone, maybe because I was so tired, maybe because I was in a dark barn with mice squeaking in the rafters and moonlight streaming through cobwebby windows—for whatever reason, the whole experience felt fraught with incantatory significance.

CONVERSION OF THE ROMAN EMPIRE

I've often tried to envision the chaotic aftermath of the Crucifixion. Fishermen and farmers who'd given up everything to follow their itinerant teacher, now suddenly abandoned and reeling with shock. And also terrified: what would happen to Jesus' loyal group? No matter what miracles they'd personally watched him perform, now he was dead, and they were sure to be next. It was not until the Resurrection began to unfold and Jesus reappeared in a new, not-so-easy-to-recognize guise— something was utterly different about his body, though he could still touch people, eat, speak like a man—that they could begin see any kind of future at all. And then, fifty days after the first stunning miracle came the second: Pentecost. Tongues of fire streamed down upon them. They were filled with the Holy Spirit. And suddenly they could speak other languages and Jesus' last words to them began to make sense: "Go, therefore, and make disciples of all nations, baptizing them in the name of the Father, and of the Son, and of the holy Spirit, teaching them to observe all that I have commanded you. And behold, I am with you always, until the end of the age" (Mt 28:19–20).

So, no doubt still shaken, they set out to fulfill this great commission. The Acts of the Apostles, which provides all the passages for the First Reading during the Easter season each year, records some of the events of these early missionary days. Those who went the farthest from Jerusalem were Peter and Philip, but eventually they were joined and then far surpassed by Paul, that once-fierce persecutor of Jesus' followers who underwent his famous conversion experience on the road to Damascus and then proceeded almost singlehandedly to spread the Gospel throughout the Roman Empire. Whereas in Jesus' day, nearly all his followers were Jews living in Israel, within two hundred years of his death there were numerous Christian communities spread from Rome to Asia Minor, many of them made up primarily of Gentile converts. Though the Epistles of the New Testament were written by several of these original apostolic missionaries (Peter, James, John, Jude), by far the majority of them (thirteen or possibly fourteen out of twenty-one, as the authorship of the Letter to the Hebrews is in some doubt) were composed by that dynamic latecomer, Paul.

These letters were not for the most part personal, in the sense of being intended for a single reader but were instead addressed to individual Christian congregations throughout the Roman Empire. As such, and even though they follow the same general pattern, each of them takes up different concerns and themes. They are at the same time eminently theological and thoroughly practical, intended to guide and lead and provide defense against the many attractive heresies circulating through the Empire. Some scholars believe that the final book in the Bible, the book of Revelation, should also be considered an epistle as it contains within it letters addressed to seven different churches.[1]

THE EPISTLES

The Epistles of the New Testament provide some of our earliest records of the infant Church. They tell the story of what happened after Jesus' Death, Resurrection, and Ascension. They continue the great family saga that began with Abram-turned-Abraham two thousand years before the birth of Christ. They show us which questions rose quickly to the top—questions that would have to be settled in the seven great Ecumenical Councils that took place between AD 325 and AD 787—and which deep concerns plagued these early groups of Christians trying to live out the teachings of their resurrected savior. That there were mighty struggles is clear. Even the two major apostles, Peter and Paul, had their differences, especially over the issue of whether Jesus came to save Gentiles too. So from the beginning, the Church was embroiled in controversy. Yet the Epistles also chronicle marvelous examples of Christ-like love—people selling all they owned and giving their money to the deacons for distribution to the poor, people healing one another in the name of Jesus.

Thus, when we come to the Second Reading of the day, we come to some of the richest passages in the Bible. Puzzling, they often are. Paul, especially, was a great visionary but also, in his pre-conversion days, a highly educated Pharisee, which means he had a steel-trap mind. Some of his letters read like scholarly treatises. Others sound like pastoral exhortations. Still others are like love letters to God. They have been pored over for centuries, have formed the basis for entire theologies, and in general are credited with providing much of the glue that held the early Church together.

THE SECOND READING

After Kathy has returned to her chair by the piano, there is a brief silence. I like these silences in the Mass, which are deliberately held even longer at the Hermitage and other monasteries. They give me time to absorb what I've just heard. They feel like active listening time.

Then Pat exits her pew on the left side of the church and walks—glides—forward. Pat, who is as slender as a teenager despite her seven grandchildren, moves like a dancer. I think she may be one of the most body-wise people I've ever met. Portuguese like Lynnette, she has the same ageless skin, the same look of impossible health. Yet three years ago when I showed up, still a little sleepy and disoriented, for early morning EM duty, she hugged me and whispered in my ear, "I have ovarian cancer. And it doesn't look good."

As it turned out, her cancer had already progressed, and suddenly one of the more extraverted women I know was undergoing multiple surgeries, then months of heavy-duty chemo. What bothered her the most was not losing her hair (half the town got together and donated money for a great-looking wig) and not the physical side effects, though they were severe. It was being confined to her house because her immune system was so compromised by the drugs that she couldn't take a chance on exposing herself to the Christmas-shopping crowds. It was having to stop herself from hugging and kissing her little grandchildren.

I went to see her during this long confinement. Always thin, she'd lost a scary amount of weight. She was bald. She was cold because she had no body fat left. And when she stood in her driveway to wave goodbye to me, bundled up as though we were in the dead of a Minnesota winter, I thought I'd never seen such a sad and lonely sight.

But now here she is, and she would be the first to say that she made it because of prayer. For a while it seemed that half the world was praying for Pat. And we were praying boldly, asking God to completely and totally heal a person already in an advanced stage of notoriously aggressive cancer. Whatever the explanation, her checkups for the past three years have shown her body to be clear of any tumors. As she stands there behind the ambo, flashing her irrepressible smile, I am pretty sure I am looking at a walking miracle.

"A reading from the Letter of Saint Paul to the Romans," she says.

> Brothers and sisters:
> You are not in the flesh;
> > on the contrary, you are in the spirit,
> > if only the Spirit of God dwells in you.
> Whoever does not have the Spirit of Christ does not
> > belong to him.
> If the Spirit of the one who raised Jesus from the
> > dead dwells in you,
> > the one who raised Christ from the dead

> will give life to your mortal bodies also,
>   through his Spirit that dwells in you.
> Consequently, brothers and sisters,
>   we are not debtors to the flesh,
>   to live according to the flesh.
> For if you live according to the flesh, you will die,
>   but if by the Spirit you put to death the deeds
>   of the body,
>   you will live.
> (Rom 8:9, 11–13)

She stops. She lets the silence go on for a moment, a skill that I'm guessing grew more developed in her during all those months of chemo and of waiting. Then she says, "The word of the Lord," and we respond with, "Thanks be to God."

FLESH VERSUS SPIRIT

This passage has made me think of Mom again. One of the many things she and I disagreed about was this very issue of flesh versus spirit. Despite being a lifetime church-goer, Mom thought you could easily get misled by Christianity if you didn't watch out. You needed to stay sharp; you needed to remember that you were primarily a human being, not a god in training. Religion in general tended to produce zealots, who were the worst sort of creatures Mom could imagine, and one way to defend yourself against that particularly insidious form of seduction was to warmly embrace this earthly life.

This meant you got a good education; you developed your mind. It meant that you pursued the gifts you had been given. If you were naturally talented at music, for example, you should study it and become as accomplished as you could possibly be, which is exactly what Tina, a professional classical pianist, has done. If you were a great cook, you should do a lot of eating and enjoy every bite—which is no doubt why all five of us siblings are unabashed foodies. To get all wrapped up in the quest for holiness—which to her meant foolish self-denial and airy-fairy notions about your own significance in the grand scheme of things—was not only dangerous but truly unattractive. She did not have an ascetical bone in her body. Needless to say, she never clicked with the monks.

I think about all the deaths I have experienced in the past couple of years in light of this passage we have just heard: "For if you live according to the flesh, you will die, but if by the Spirit you put to death the deeds of your body, you will live" (Rom 8:13). For a moment, I am filled with bleakness. Does this mean that my earth-loving, practical mother, who cast such a suspicious eye on what she viewed as religious pretentiousness, lived strictly by the flesh? Certainly, she resented any implication that we should be focusing on the invisible and the ephemeral; certainly, she was wary of investing herself in religious mystery over day-to-day living. And certainly, she did not let go of daily life very easily. A week before she entered into her final struggle with metastasized liver cancer, just after I had helped her to the commode and she realized that she was feeling a little better that morning, she gave me one of her defiant-child looks. "Somebody," she said, "might be pretty surprised one of these days."

"Surprised at what?" I asked.

"At the fact that I might just be sticking around a lot longer than somebody seems to think I will."

"Mom," I sighed. "Oh, Mom."

But as all of us must at some point, she died, and I wonder—every day I wonder—how it has gone for her in the new kind of existence she is experiencing now. I wonder if her kind and generous heart, her open door to the world, her deep and abiding interest in all of God's creation, her ebullient sense of gratitude—all of which made her a moral exemplar for many—were her way of "putting to death the deeds of the flesh," by which, of course, Paul meant sin.

I reach for Mike's hand, resting open beside me on the pew. I realize that I am suddenly identifying one of the sources of my lingering sadness these past months. Because I simply can't know what has happened to my mother. And that is a mystery almost too difficult to bear.

I wish I could send her a letter, ask her what she thinks of God, now that she's met him face-to-face. I'd like her to write me a letter back and tell me all about it.

Resurrecting

The Alleluia, the Gospel Reading

Somewhere in the back of the church, a small child screeches. This is not the normal thing at 7:30 a.m. Mass; the Children's Liturgy happens at 9:00 a.m., so that's when most people bring their children. I can hear the young parents shushing their toddler, and I feel sorry for them. It's hard to bring your kids to church when they are so young. I hope the parents understand that even though their little ones sometimes can't help disrupting Mass, having them here is a real gift.

Given this lingering wistfulness of mine, I am exceedingly grateful for my own grandkids, who can always, no matter what, take me straight out of myself and into a better land. Not just Sophie and Eli, the ones who live close enough to accompany us to Mass, but Benjamin and Christopher too, three and a half hours to the south— along with our godchildren Jack, Abbey Jane, and Laney May, who—even though they have a perfectly good set of grandparents in Michigan—have elected to call us Grandpa and Grandma, which we consider a great honor indeed. These seven (I think of them as the seven dwarves) not only bring the exuberance of my own childhood back to me but have taught me an awful lot about God. And considering that they range in age from three to thirteen, I find this both remarkable and impressive.

The first of them to stick his finger in the God-socket was Ben. At four months, he was already obsessed with the gold cross I wore around my neck. He would twist the chain around his finger, put the cross between his pink gums, and then rest his forehead against mine and stare into my eyes from a quarter inch away, as though asking for an explanation of the powerful religious sentiments that were so obviously coursing through him. It was disconcerting. The first word out of his mouth was, not surprisingly, "Cross!" Always with an exclamation point. And then, as he was driven around town in his car seat, he began spotting crosses on top of churches: "Cross and church! Cross and church!"

At two, he was already practicing the Lord's Prayer with his dad at night, and one morning his mom caught him on the back porch, preaching to the birds like a miniature Saint Francis. When I took him inside the Old Mission in San Luis Obispo for the first time, he stood as if paralyzed by emotions he couldn't begin to sort out, much less to name, then weakly pointed up at the gigantic crucifix above the altar as though that would explain everything. And Ben's deep spiritual sensibilities have been echoed in countless ways by his fellow dwarves: Eli's five-year-old crow of incredulous joy when Aslan came back to life at the end of C. S. Lewis's *The Lion, the Witch, and the*

Wardrobe; Sophie's fervent three-year-old prayers for the safety of all animals; eight-year-old Laney May's laser-like questions about forgiveness; Christopher's request for pomegranate juice and a chunk of bread so the kids could hold their own church service in the treehouse.

THE RELIGIOUS POTENTIAL OF CHILDREN

I do not believe our grandchildren are unique; most kids seem to be spiritually more alive than your average adult, at least before the world has its way with them. In *The Religious Potential of the Child*, scholar and educator Sofia Cavalletti, for example, observes that a child is a creature who "moves with ease in the world of the transcendent and who delights in—satisfied and serene—the contact with God."[1] Believing that "the religious experience is fundamentally an expression of love," she concludes that religion thus "corresponds in a special way to the child's nature."[2] Encouraged by a colleague of Maria Montessori, Cavalletti developed a program of Christian formation for very young and sometimes war-traumatized children in Italy in the early 1950s. Called the Catechesis of the Good Shepherd, it was designed to recognize and encourage what she called "the religious potential of the child." Catechist Rebekah Rojcewicz, in her foreword to Cavalletti's book, explains that children not only have a natural propensity toward relationship with God but can even become religious exemplars for adults. "What does Jesus mean by 'mere children'?" she asks. "The Jerusalem Bible notes that he was referring to the disciples, whom he also called 'little ones'; but I believe he was also referring to children in the literal sense . . . when he placed a child in their midst and said that one must receive the kingdom like a child."[3]

I know that the seven dwarves have at times served as my own spiritual guides. For as hard as it is to admit, my usual modus operandi is anything but open, trusting, and childlike—even, sad to say, at Mass. Too often, I'm carting along my list of "Very Important Things to Work Out While in Church." Too often, I come weighed down by All My Responsibilities. Too often, in short, I come to Mass like some kind of doleful Eeyore instead of in the way Christ calls me to come: like Ben, like Chris, like Eli and Sophie. Like Jack and Abbey Jane and Laney May. Like a happy-go-lucky kid.

Which is not to idealize kids-and-church. Over the past five years, we have taken our grandkids to Mass many times, beginning with Eli as a two-year-old and eventually Sophie at eighteen months. During the service they are of course naturally bored and sleepy at times, but at other moments, clearly riveted—no dutiful listening for them. I watch their eyes being caught by the light through the stained glass windows, by the flicker of candles on the altar, by the golden gleam along the edges of the Book of the Gospels. They crane their necks to watch Peter processing down the aisle with the crucifix. Quietly and curiously, they watch people at prayer. They kneel and try it themselves, resting their faces in their hands as the old folks do. What I see in them when they are in church is phenomenology in the flesh. They are thoroughly experiencing their experience. There is no intellectual screen between them and what is unfolding before their eyes. I'm pretty sure this kind of absolute and unafraid openness was what Jesus was referring to when he said, "Amen, I say to you, unless you turn and become like children, you will not enter the kingdom of heaven" (Mt 18:3).

Lay your burdens aside, in other words, even if you have to pick them up again in an hour. Stop taking yourself so seriously. Remember that the world will continue to spin without you in charge. Raise your face to the shower of light.

THE ALLELUIA

Kathy, who is back behind her music stand, raises her arms. We stand to sing the "Celtic Alleluia," a twentieth-century version of one of the most venerable elements of the Mass. The word *alleluia* itself is derived from the Hebrew *Hallelu Jah*, which means "Praise ye, Ya." *Ya* is a shortened version of *Yahweh*, one of the oldest names for God. In ancient Hebrew times, it was spoken out loud only by priests and only on special occasions. The Alleluia announces the high point of the Liturgy of the Word—the Gospel reading—and it is a way for the congregation to greet Yahweh-the-Lord with thanksgiving, joy, and a cry of triumph.

Perhaps because the Alleluia fills such an important role during the Mass, by the ninth century it was undergoing extensive ornamentation. These additions were called *tropes*, and they could take several forms. One might be a new *melisma*, or a single syllable extended through a whole series of notes (a good example would be the long drawn-out "Gloria" in the Christmas carol "Angels We Have Heard on High") Another might be the addition of new words to an already existing melisma. A third could be a new verse consisting of both text and music. Why would a composer trope? It was his way of creating musical art while still working within the tight structure of liturgical chant.[4]

The Alleluia of today is a simpler thing than it was during the heyday of troping. The "Celtic Alleluia" in particular, which was originally composed by a twentieth-century Irish composer named Fintan O'Carroll and later rearranged by Christopher Walker, harkens back to village processions and the slapping of farmers' boots on muddy roads. There's an arm-swinging rhythm to it. You can smell the sea and the moors. And even if Kathy did not signal the congregation to rise at this point, you would quite naturally jump to your feet because there is no happier music in all of the Mass than the "Celtic Alleluia." It even trumps the Gloria in this regard.

THE GOSPEL READING

Once we have sung the triple Alleluia refrain—"Al-le-lu-ia, al-le-lu-ia, al-le-lu-ia"—she sings today's verse: "Blessed are you, Father, Lord of heaven and earth; you have revealed to little ones the mysteries of the kingdom." Meanwhile, Father Ken rises from his chair, prays silently for God to be in his heart and on his lips, walks to the altar, and lifts the Book of the Gospels high over his head, displaying it to every section of the church before proceeding to the ambo. There, he ceremoniously places the Book, opening it to the reading for the day, and says, "The Lord be with you."

We respond: "And with your spirit."

He says, "A reading from the holy Gospel according to Matthew."

We reply, "Glory to you, O Lord."

If we were at the Hermitage right now, Father Ken would be handed a *thurible*, or smoking metal censer on a chain, and would use it to make three double swings around the book. The practice of censing goes way back in the history of the Church, and though some ancient customs were indeed dropped after Vatican II, the *Roman Missal* as revised in 1969 continued to allow incense at any Mass, regardless of setting or occasion. Nowadays you are more likely to see it done at monasteries than at parish churches, however—perhaps because it makes some people sneeze. Like genuflection, for Mike and me it seems a particularly foreign Catholic practice given our pasts. But I have come to love the "scent of prayer" it conveys—that exotic, caravansary odor produced by multiple layers of incense smoldering on lit charcoal—along with the fact that every important item in the Mass, including the congregation, including me, gets censed at some point whenever a thurible (carried by a thurifer) is present. The ancient Greek root of this odd word means "to sacrifice."

Without incense, Father Ken makes the Sign of the Cross over the Book of the Gospels with a flat hand held sideways, like the blade of a knife, and then joins the rest of us as, employing our thumbs in a markedly unmodern way, we make the same sign on our foreheads, lips, and chests. This ancient warning signal to Satan to stay far away also means, according to Joseph Jungmann, that we are pledging the following: "For the word which Christ brought and which is set down in this book we are willing to stand up with a mind that is open; we are ready to confess it with our mouth; and above all we are determined to safeguard it faithfully in our hearts."[5]

We will remain standing, as Catholics have stood since time immemorial, throughout the entire reading of the Gospel. Before the days of pews in churches, people used to support themselves through the Mass on wooden sticks or canes, but during the Gospel readings, these were cast aside, along with every male head covering, including crowns. During medieval times when armed knights were sometimes in attendance, it was common for them to lay aside their weapons, cloaks, and gloves at this point. In other places, knights would place their hands on the hilts of their swords or even draw their blades and extend them outward during the Gospel reading as a sign of their willingness to fight and die for Christ.[6] I think about our own St. Patrick's "knights," the mostly gray-headed and always amiable Knights of Columbus who not only cook and serve at our Lenten fish fries but who, as a national organization, contributed more than 170 million dollars to charities such as Habitat for Humanity, Special Olympics, and worldwide disaster relief in 2013. Still fighting the good fight.

Father Ken begins to read:

> At that time Jesus exclaimed:
> "I give praise to you, Father, Lord of heaven and earth,
>   for although you have hidden these things
>   from the wise and the learned
>   you have revealed them to little ones.
> Yes, Father, such has been your gracious will.
> All things have been handed over to me by my Father.
> No one knows the Son except the Father,
>   and no one knows the Father except the Son
>   and anyone to whom the Son wishes to reveal him.
>
> "Come to me, all you who labor and are burdened,
>   and I will give you rest.
> Take my yoke upon you and learn from me,
>   for I am meek and humble of heart;
>   and you will find rest for yourselves.
> For my yoke is easy, and my burden light."
> (Mt 11:25–30)

Then Father Ken leans over, kisses the Book, lifts it high and proclaims, "The Gospel of the Lord," and we respond with, "Praise to you, Lord Jesus Christ," and once more take our seats.

THE INNOCENCE OF CHILDREN

The Gospel reading has made me think about the seven dwarves ("for although you have hidden these things from the wise and the learned you have revealed them to little ones"), realizing that not only do these beloved grandchildren and godchildren lift me out of my broodiness but they also contribute to it. They are still, even at the advanced ages of the oldest of them—eleven and thirteen—so beautiful, so innocent, so utterly dependent upon the love, strength, and faith of their elders. I worry about the world that we are bequeathing to them. How will they cope with the spreading malignancy of radical Islamism? How will they stop the temperature of the earth from rising beyond habitable levels? How will they prevent pandemics of super-viruses and antibiotic-resistant bacteria? How will they feed the hungry, care for the widow and orphan, clothe the naked, when their own lives may be so much harder than ours have been? The plain fact is that I don't know. I pray for them, envisioning the seven of them standing within a circle of light, and I mentally make the Sign of the Cross—beware Satan!—over their trusting young faces, but honestly, I don't know. For at times the troubles of our times seem so beyond fixing that I wonder why I am praying at all.

It helps, then, to remember those medieval knights with outstretched swords, listening intently to the good news before going off to die in battle. It helps to remember those brave catechumens of the early church, training in secret to become baptized Christians and very likely martyrs at the same time. It helps to remember the Black Death and self-disregarding saints like Catherine of Siena, who devoted all her energy and strength to those dying of the plague. For if the world is hard now, and it is, then truly it is no harder for the people who live in it—or for those who will live on in it after me, like those much-loved grandchildren of mine—than it has ever been. Jesus came into what can be a very dark place indeed.

Which is exactly why he came. This is difficult for me to remember at times—that Christ came to dispel the darkness—but if not for that, then what? I think of the Benedictus chanted at the Hermitage during Lauds, the morning prayer that celebrates the beginning of a new day, "Blessed be the Lord, the God of Israel. He has come to his people and set them free. He has raised up for us a mighty savior, born of the house of his servant David. . . . In the tender compassion of our God, the dawn from on high shall break upon us, to shine on those who dwell in darkness and the shadow of death, and to guide our feet into the way of peace" (Lk 1:68–79).

I pray that it be so.

Listening

The Homily

Thinking about the kids and church has made me think about my own childhood religious experience. What I remember most about the Lutheran services of the fifties and sixties were the magnificent Reformation-era hymns, so many of them of German origin in spite of our being a mostly Scandinavian congregation. Though we did not have a real pipe organ until I was in high school, our organist was a professional musician. If there is one thing I miss about my Lutheran childhood, it is those wonderful hymns, which often triggered an intense experience of God's presence.

THE PRIMACY OF PREACHING

Not so much, however, the long sermons that accompanied them—that were, in fact, the main point of our being in church. Not that the sermons weren't powerful, for they often were, but they struck me at a completely different level than the hymns did, at the level of thinking instead of experiencing. Lutheranism, like Presbyterianism and most contemporary Evangelicalism, was founded on the principle of *sola scriptura*, or scripture as the only true authority for individual Christians, which meant that the Word, both spoken and written, took precedence in our life of faith. Such early Reformers as Martin Luther and John Calvin believed that it was dangerous to allow what Catholics had always referred to as Sacred Tradition much room at the Christian table (Sacred Tradition would include all sacraments beyond Baptism and Eucharist; the hierarchy of priests, bishops, cardinals, and popes; the liturgy; and the teachings of the Church Fathers, among other things). If the Bible were indeed the only source of truth, ways of worship that had been established over the centuries could be safely dispensed with, for, as Luther declared, "A single layman armed with Scripture is greater than the mightiest pope without it."

In Protestant denominations—even a liturgical one like Lutheranism—that took sola scriptura to heart, the sermon (not the Eucharist) thus became the centerpiece of the worship service, with the pulpit often becoming the primary focus of attention. Sermons were meant to "break open the Word," to teach, to explain. The goal was to produce educated, independent lay people who could take their Bibles home, study them, and learn how to live upright Christian lives. And (perhaps somewhat ironically, given the Protestant rejection of the authority of the priests) we relied on our pastors to translate the hard parts for us.

In spite of my preference for the hymns over sermons, I grew up admiring preachers. My Uncle Ivan, for example, was a Lutheran pastor who spent fifteen years as a missionary in Japan. When he and my aunt and cousins came home on furlough, he would be invited to preach at one of the big churches that helped support mission work. At ten, I remember being enraptured by the fact that my uncle was the guy in the pulpit.

My sister Gretchen married a Baptist minister from England, an articulate and erudite young man with the classiest accent any of us had ever heard. Only in his twenties when he came to America, John now pastors one of the larger nondenominational churches in the country. When he preaches, he strides back and forth in his suit and tie while the members of his huge congregation take notes in their Bibles.

Over the years, I've been to large Presbyterian churches where ministers deliver sermons in their doctoral robes and to Free Churches in Scotland where homespun pastors speak authoritatively from the pulpit for forty-five minutes straight. I've visited Episcopalian churches where robed women priests deliver elegant sermons full of literary allusions and neo-Reformed churches where scruffily bearded thirty-two-year-olds in jeans, untucked shirts, and sandals pronounce with enormous verve on the book of Hosea for most of an hour.

I tell you, it's impressive, all the preaching that goes on out there.

THE HOMILY VERSUS THE SERMON

But it wasn't until I went to my first Mass that a heretofore unacknowledged disquiet regarding the primacy of place so often given to the sermon during Protestant worship finally snapped into focus for me. For the first time in my life, I was in a service not dominated by the preaching. Not only was I no longer so focused on the personality of the pastor, I found that I remembered that Mass afterward in a way I usually did not remember the main points of sermons, no matter how entertaining or instructive. This was a whole new world, and part of it was the fact that the homily, as it is called in the Catholic church, is comparatively brief in the grand scheme of the Mass. Fifteen minutes long at most, it is there in support of the First and Second Readings, the Responsorial Psalm, and the Gospel. Or as the General Instruction of the *Roman Missal* puts it, "The homily is not an isolated example of biblical interpretation or a purely academic exercise. It is directed from faith, that of the Church and of the ordained minister who preaches in the name of Christ and his Church, to faith—that is, the faith of the Christian community gathered in a spirit of prayer and praise in the presence of the Risen Christ."[1]

The word *homily* is derived from the Greek word *homilia*, meaning "to have communion or hold verbal intercourse with a person." Since the third century, the term has been associated with an informal commentary on some part of scripture with the goal of teasing out both the literal and spiritual meanings of the passage. The word *sermon*, on the other hand, finds its root in the

Latin *sermo*, which means "discourse." A sermon is more like an oration in that it is often more formally structured than a homily and frequently includes sections devoted to exposition, exhortation, and practical application. Of the two, the sermon is clearly more concerned with doctrinal teaching. The homily, in contrast, is meant to shed light on the readings for the day.

Thus, from very early times it has been the duty of the homilist "above all to find, by his own efforts, the proper medium between the language of the people and the pretensions of the more highly educated."[2] This means that the homily was generally preached in the vernacular—a tradition that continued all the way up to Vatican II, after which the entire Order of Mass was translated into the native languages of its international parishes. As Joseph Jungmann says about the ancient homiletic tradition, "There was from olden times a definite and restrictive pattern for the spiritual talk that followed on the reading, a pattern exacted by the circumstances in which it appeared. The talk was to be about the word of God that had been read from the Sacred Scriptures, it was not to stifle it but apply it to the present day." Then he adds, somewhat dryly, "This neither is nor was the spot to unfold the entire preaching of the Church."[3]

What is common to both homily and its lengthier cousin, however, is often a central anecdote or story. Why? Stories in their purest form are as old as the human race. Though nowadays, especially when they are told in church, they are often employed as rhetorical devices to help make a point, this was not their original function.

We first became enthralled with stories because they are so interesting.

Perhaps this is why Jesus relied so heavily on the parable. The tale of the prodigal son or the lost sheep or the widow's mite is easier for most people to understand than theological explication. Stories are about concrete situations; they are grounded in real life; they have the credentials of particularity. Thus, they have the ability to unify us by stirring in us mutual concern for the characters involved. Will the miffed older brother in the prodigal son story ever get over himself and welcome his wayward sibling home? Will the shepherd ever find the sheep? Will the much-abused vineyard owner ever obtain justice?

FATHER KEN'S HOMILY

So it is no surprise that Father Ken begins today's homily with a story. He tells us about Rachel, a literature student back in the days when he was a New Orleans professor rather than a priest, who went on to become a successful pediatrician. He says, "I still consider her to be the 'prophet' among my students." The daughter of an African-American mother and a Jewish father, she was raised as a Catholic who had a firm moral foundation to her life. She was also clearly brilliant. When she responded to a question raised in the class, "there would be a stillness in the room that was palpable." Her peers listened respectfully to her because her insights were somewhat amazing in one so young. Yet she was neither grandstanding nor trying to show off. Father Ken says, "She was just a very smart person who did not hide her gifts under a bushel basket of false humility. What she knew, she shared, and we were all grateful for the gift of her sharing."

As I am wondering how the story of Rachel connects with the Gospel reading for the day, Father Ken suggests that Rachel had something in common with Jesus. He, too, had obvious powers and gifts that he neither flaunted nor hid. They were simply aspects of his person, and it was in part because of them that people were not only willing to listen to him, even when he spoke harsh certitudes, but also to believe in what he said and to allow his words to transform their hearts. His primary message, however, was surrender, which means, says Father Ken, "that we are to allow the Spirit of God to lead us." Yet surrender is not as easy as it sounds because we are not used to being led by the humble.

He now moves to the most famous line of the Gospel passage for today. Christ tells us it is safe to surrender our all to him because his yoke is easy and his burden light. I have thought about this line for years, especially during rough times when it is difficult not to cave into anger or despair, wondering how, exactly, Jesus can describe the Christian way as "easy." Somehow, we are not only supposed to bear undeserved suffering with noble patience, but we are supposed to continue, right through the middle of it, thinking more of others than ourselves. Not only is that not natural and easy, it seems completely impossible. But what Father Ken seems to be saying here is that it is not difficult situations themselves that are the problem for us but instead our need to control what is going on. And when we give up our plans and strategies, when we let go of our fierce desire to know all there is to know about the mysterious future, then Jesus himself will start carrying our burdens for us. They will be in his hands, not ours. Our job is simply to trust that, out of love for us, he will never drop them.

Hmm. At some level, I remain suspicious. I think about that other line in this Gospel passage we have just heard, the one that calls us to become like little children. If I am honest, this description of what true faith is like—childlike wonder and trustfulness—raises instant resistance in me. Though, like Maria Montessori and Sofia Cavalletti, I am fascinated by kids, I am far too used to shouldering heavy responsibility to fall very easily for this invitation to surrender myself. And as a Norwegian Midwesterner to the bones despite a lifetime in laid-back California, I cannot imagine giving up strength for voluntary weakness.

Which might, I am starting to see, have something significant to do with my gray funk. Maybe I am just really, really tired. It's been a (I confess it) grueling few years, what with caring for the sick and dying older generation while at the same time helping to raise a brand-new one. And I myself am no spring chicken; it takes more these days to schlepp the weight of the world around. Maybe, in fact, it is finally time to take the invitation seriously. Maybe this is one of the reasons I am supposed to be at Mass today.

At the end of the homily, Father Ken reads Gerard Manley Hopkins's great poem "God's Grandeur." I love this poem, but I, too, taught English literature, and I know that it utterly baffles most folks. This would not bother in the least the nineteenth-century Jesuit Hopkins, who never expected his poetry to see print and who would probably collapse in shock to hear it quoted from a pulpit. But I wonder about the hard-working, not-necessarily-academic folks of St. Patrick's parish. What do they find in it, other than the beautiful sound of its strange, sometimes made-up words?

I glance surreptitiously at my fellow parishioners. And I see that they are all, to a person, listening as intently as birds listen when somebody is crunching through the forest beneath them. Take heed! Take heed! Then Father Ken ties it all together—Rachel, Hopkins, and the easy yoke—with the last line of the poem. Why is it safe for us to surrender? "Because the Holy Ghost over the bent World broods with warm breast and ah! bright wings."[4]

My eyes fill, and I sneak a finger under my glasses to rub them dry before my tears can embarrass me. It's true; I am emotionally beat. And I want to hand off all that sad worry to someone else, someone strong enough to bear it. I want to stop having anxious dreams about people who are waiting for me to help them while I am caught up in an increasingly frustrating and confusing web of lost car keys, misplaced wallet, disappeared phone, forgotten facts, and incoming Pacific storms. I want, I really do want, to finally surrender. I sneak another finger under my glasses, scrubbing fiercely at my wet eyes.

Perhaps, I think, this is what Catholic homilies—so brief and informal compared to the weighty sermons I heard as a Lutheran child—are meant to do. Not so much to teach the Bible as to throw swinging bridges between the readings for the day. Not so much to be a moral exhortation as an invitation to go deeper into the mysterious realm of the heart. Not so much to impart doctrine but to herald what is coming next: the great sacrifice and celebration of the Eucharist.

"Take heed! Take heed!" they proclaim.

Declaring

The Profession of Faith

Father Ken, his homily delivered, is back in his presider's chair, sitting in silence with his head bowed. Knowing him as well as I do, you'd think I could guess at what is going on inside his mind at this moment, whether he is praying or evaluating what he just said or simply resting. But I am clueless. Father Ken in his green chasuble is considerably more mysterious than the dear friend with whom I used to teach. He is acting *in persona Christi Capitis* and, surrounded as he is by the symbols of faith—the crucifix, the altar, the burning tapers—he occupies the central space in an ancient icon.

I find myself once again thinking of the first Mass I ever attended—how nervous I was and yet how drawn. After that initial experience I began slipping into Masses whenever I got the chance. At first I felt very out of place: I recognized some of the words of the liturgy from my Lutheran childhood but not all; I had no idea why people were crossing themselves at particular points; I was afraid of offending people (thanks, Midwestern gene pool) by getting it wrong. After enough time in church, however, I started to feel more comfortable and even moved a few rows closer to the altar.

Better yet, I found myself looking forward to seeing certain people at Mass, as if they had become my secret friends, though the words we exchanged were almost always confined to "good morning" and "peace be with you." None of these secret friends of mine seemed miffed that a sheepish-looking non-Catholic was hanging around watching everything they did. They seemed to understand that I couldn't help myself. I suspected that a couple of them might even be praying for me—that they had figured out I was going through a spiritual crisis of some kind. At one point, a kind pew-mate showed me how to find the Order of Mass in the front of the *Breaking Bread* missal. Now I could make the appropriate responses, which made me feel less like an alien.

Except, that is, when it came to the Creed, which we were supposed to recite after the homily for the day. It's not that I didn't know the Creed; I'd memorized the Apostles' Creed as a child. It wasn't even that I objected to some particular statement in it; a few of these were tricky to decipher, true, but there was nothing obviously objectionable in any of them. Publicly and formally declaring my newly rediscovered belief in God, however, was still just too scary. I'd been away from church for so many years, nearly twenty, and I'd said so many flippant or even downright malicious things about religious believers during that time away that the Creed genuinely spooked me. It was so straightforward, so unswerving, so absolute.

Truly, how could a person know for sure that she believed every single word of such an ancient and official-sounding document?

So I fudged. I would stand with everyone else; I would fold my hands solemnly across my middle and gaze at the crucifix as if transfixed. Then, while everyone around me made their firm declarations, I would whisper, "I believe in (murmur, murmur, murmur). And in Jesus Christ (murmur, murmur, murmur)." That seemed to work. At least until the point I began going to RCIA classes, where I knew I could no longer waffle if I were really going to enter the Catholic Church.

HISTORY OF THE CREED

Professions of faith beginning with the word *credo* ("I believe" in Latin) were first composed for catechumens to recite on the day of their baptisms. Especially during the era of persecution prior to AD 313, it was critical that new members knew what they believed as it was quite possible they would at some point be hauled before a tribunal and ordered to renounce their faith under threat of torture and execution. It was likely that these early creeds were not written down at all but instead memorized by catechumens when they were deemed ready. Up until that point in their training, the content of these creeds was considered to be too sacred and mysterious for them to hear.

The Apostles' Creed, which is the shorter of the two credos used today, is older than the more complex Nicene Creed. Legend has it that the Apostles' Creed was composed by none other than the twelve apostles on the day of the Pentecost, each of them writing one of its twelve articles. More likely, however, is that the Apostles' Creed as we know it today grew out of these earlier baptismal creeds. By the year AD 180 or so it began to appear in written form. The first official mention of it is in a letter, probably written by Saint Ambrose, from the Council of Milan to Pope Siricius in AD 390. The Creed itself is simple, straightforward, and clearly reflects Gospel statements regarding the three Persons of the Trinity: God the Creator, Christ the Redeemer, and Holy Spirit the Sanctifier. It does not, however, specifically mention the nature of Christ, a subject that became an increasingly hot topic during the third and fourth centuries as the Church worked out its Christological doctrine. Today, the Apostles' Creed is most often used by the Church for catechizing children.

The Nicene Creed came into being after the First Council of Nicaea in AD 325, the Council of Constantinople in 381, and the Council of Chalcedon in 451. Though there were seven of these Ecumenical Councils, these three in particular were meant to settle ongoing disputes about Christ's nature, disputes that were imperiling the unity of the still-young Church. For example, a faction called the Ebionites believed that Jesus was nothing but a man. The Gnostic Docetics, however, were sure that he was not a man at all but pure spirit in the illusory guise of a human being. The Monothelites believed that he had two separate natures, divine and human, but only one will.

Possibly the most difficult position of all was the one held by the gospel writers, the apostles, and the earliest Christians. Called the doctrine of the hypostatic union, it says the Word of God came down from heaven and was incarnated as the man we call Jesus, who had both a human and a divine nature that were united, in the words of the Council of Chalcedon, "without confusion, change, division or separation. The distinction between the natures was never abolished by their union, but rather the character proper to each of the two natures was preserved as they came together in one person (*prosopon*) and one hypostasis" (quoted in *CCC*, 467). Any deviation from this bedrock belief, its defenders were convinced, was bound to lead first to divisive error, and then to the loss of the faith itself.

HERESY

Ideas about fundamentals of the faith that had been definitively deemed erroneous by the Councils were thereafter called *heresies*, and teachers who persisted in teaching unorthodox beliefs despite the Church's opposition were called *heretics*. However, the enormous cultural amalgam contained within the third- and fourth-century Roman Empire continued to produce far more fascinating heresies than *The Da Vinci Code*. Gnosticism, one of the most persistent, is still alive and well today, thanks in part to the 1945 discovery of a fourth-century collection of scrolls in the Egyptian desert; the Nag Hammadi Library, as it is called, contains several "gospels" written by Gnostic authors who lived between the second and fourth centuries, and contemporary fans of Gnosticism are convinced that herein lies the real truth about Jesus and his mission.

Unlike our era, so committed to tolerance that we hardly dare disagree with one another for fear of giving offense, during the centuries that encompassed the great Christological debates, people often paid a high personal price for their beliefs. Depending on who was in power at the time, you could be exiled, imprisoned, tortured, or executed for your theological views. And these controversies continued to swirl for centuries.

One of the most persistent was Arianism (so named after its proponent, the presbyter Arius, and not to be confused with Aryanism), which proposed that Christ was a Being created by God out of nothing before the beginning of the world, and thus an inferior, secondary god, certainly not co-equal to the Creator himself. Arianism was incompatible with belief in the Holy Trinity, God's life as three loving and continually interacting divine Persons in one Being.[1] Catholic Christianity firmly opposed Arianism in all its forms, staking its claim on the fact that the gospels refer over and over to Jesus not only as divine but as co-equal to God the Father. He is called "Son of God," the "Word [who] was with God and the Word [who] was God" (Jn 1:1). He clearly states, "The Father and I are one," (Jn 10:30) and "Amen, amen, I say to you, before Abraham came to be, I AM" (Jn 8:58). The word *consubstantial* in the Creed refers to this co-equality with God the Father.

No doubt the most famous opponent of Arianism was Saint Athanasius. His steadfast resistance to any effort to "demote" Christ, however, meant that each time the political winds shifted, he found himself once more in exile. Yet for him, nothing was more important than standing for the truth, no matter what the cost. Perhaps this was because of what he saw as a child. In the year AD 303, when Athanasius was only about five years old, the last great persecution against Christians was launched by Emperor Diocletian. It did not end until 311, which meant that for most of his formative years, he had watched fellow believers being hunted down and put to death for refusing to renounce their faith in the Son of God. Because of his adamant resistance to any softening of the original Gospel view of Jesus, he became known to following generations through a proverb: *Athanasius contra mundum*, or "Athanasius against the world." He is widely regarded as the savior of the Christian faith during an era when it might have been diluted beyond repair by competing heretical sects.[2]

Despite how much the Church owes to heroes like the unshakeable Athanasius, however, theological stubbornness can also be a curse. A still-unresolved—and in some people's minds, superfluous—theological disagreement continues to impede reconciliation between Catholic and Orthodox Christians (that is, Latin-speaking and Greek-speaking Christians). In AD 589 at the Third Council of Toledo, a single phrase known as the *filioque* was added to the Creed. The addition appears in the section about the Holy Spirit, who (it states) "proceeds from the Father *and the Son*" rather than the Father alone (italics mine). These three little words have had an impact far beyond their size in the thousand-year-old, still-unresolved split between the Western and Eastern Church. Though Catholic theologian Luke Timothy Johnson believes the phrase was unnecessary and should never have been added in the first place, he roundly condemns the centuries of dispute that have followed in its wake. "Here we have a great and bitter battle, all the more savage because it is between family members and over such a minor point. . . . Here we see disputants insisting on being 'right' even at the expense of being 'unrighteous.'"[3]

Even today, questions about the nature of Christ, supposedly long settled by the Christological statements of the Creed, continue to crop up. Every Christmas and Easter season seems to invite a new magazine cover story about "who Jesus really was," with tantalizing speculations about whether he might actually have been the secret husband of Mary Magdalene, a shy carpenter thrust unwillingly onto the national stage by those seeking to make religious hay, or even a Palestinian guerrilla working to undermine the Roman Empire. But after all these centuries, it is still Athanasius who gives us in the clearest possible terms the very same answer spoken by Peter when Jesus asked him, "But who do you say I am?" "You are the Messiah," Peter responded, "the Son of the Living God" (Mt 16:16).

RECITING THE CREED

And now Father Ken, who has maintained some moments of silence after giving his homily, rises to lead us in this ancient credo of the faith:

I believe in one God,
the Father almighty,
maker of heaven and earth,
of all things visible and invisible.

I believe in one Lord Jesus Christ,
the Only Begotten Son of God,
born of the Father before all ages.
God from God, Light from Light,
true God from true God,
begotten, not made, consubstantial with the Father;
For us men and for our salvation
he came down from heaven
[here, we bow until the next section begins]
and by the Holy Spirit was incarnate of the Virgin Mary,
and became man.

For our sake he was crucified under Pontius Pilate,
he suffered death and was buried,
and rose again on the third day
in accordance with the Scriptures.
He ascended into heaven
and is seated at the right hand of the Father.
He will come again in glory
to judge the living and the dead
and his kingdom will have no end.

I believe in the Holy Spirit, the Lord, the giver of life,
who proceeds from the Father and the Son,
who with the Father and the Son is adored and glorified,
who has spoken through the prophets.

I believe in one, holy, catholic and apostolic Church.
I confess one Baptism for the forgiveness of sins
and I look forward to the resurrection of the dead
and the life of the world to come. Amen.

Since those early days of RCIA, when I could only murmur the Creed, I have come to anticipate this part of the Mass, this standing together with my fellow parishioners and reciting the ancient credo of the faith. I used to wonder why it was so hard for me back then, but now I know the answer: for me, coming back to the Church after twenty years was almost like abandoning home, where I knew all the rules, in order to go live on my own in a completely foreign land. Thanks to the university culture in which I'd been formed, I'd learned to equate my sense of personhood with the intellectual positions I took. In a strange way, "I" equaled my thoughts. Thus, I'd learned to be extremely wary of being "talked into" anything without fully understanding what I was acquiescing to, much less professing a belief in mysteries so profound that even really smart people can't quite put them into words. After enough time in this strange new land, however, I began to appreciate how well those ancient bishops at those ancient Councils had articulated what is essentially ineffable. And I began to love the Creed—even the parts that push my mind into such starry regions that I am left standing mute.

Do I understand all of it? No. Do I believe it? I am trying. Or at the very least, I am praying the prayer of the father seeking healing for a son bound by an evil spirit: "Lord, I believe. Help thou my unbelief."

Interceding

The Universal Prayer, or Prayer of the Faithful

As the last words of the Creed are spoken, I can see Pat leaving the pew that seats her husband, son, daughter-in-law, and three grandkids, and making her way to the ambo. The Universal Prayer, during which we pray for, among other things, the sick and the dead, is about to begin, and suddenly I am thinking of the long string of deaths, beginning almost ten years ago, that have been making me so sad. I was in my early fifties, and the first person to die was a barrel-chested, life-loving, natural-born hermit just a little older than I am whose only goal in life, he once confided, was holiness. Father Romuald wanted to become a *staretz*, which is the Russian name for "wise and holy elder." About six months after that conversation, I ran into him at the bookstore at New Camaldoli Hermitage, where he lived. Overnight, it seemed, he'd gone cross-eyed. He noticed me noticing the cattywhumpus state of his gaze and winced. "What's going on?" I asked him. "What's happened to you?"

"I've got a tumor," he said. "Right there." And he pointed to the space between his eyebrows.

"Since when?" I asked.

"Since a couple of days ago. I woke up and there it was."

"Is it serious?"

"They don't know yet. They're going to be doing some tests."

A year later, he was dead. In between, his body slowly filled up with tumors (one of them, on his hiney, he fondly called Rosie). Though at first he tried to keep his many friends informed about the treatments he was undergoing and what, if anything, he was learning about the spiritual life during this long ordeal, eventually he got fed up with the job of emailing everybody and even more with the cancer drugs, and he told his doctors he was done. So they sent him back to his monastic cell to die, which he did with enormous fortitude and, well, holiness.

That was a hard death for those he left behind. It's always hard when the world loses a really fine person. But at least I knew that he was ready for it when it came. That he was facing it like a monk. That everything about the way he had lived his life had finally come together when he really needed to call on it.

Still, it was a loss. Then Emily, my age, had the devastating stroke that left her bed- and wheelchair-ridden. After Emily came Janet, intrepid backpacker and horsewoman, a year younger than I am, who started gimping and falling at strange moments—MS. Though both of them survived, some kind of death had taken place.

Others followed Romuald right on to the grave. There was Judy, who got lung cancer—where had it come from? She had never smoked—and Steve, not yet fifty, whose heart gave out while he was watching a basketball game, and nineteen-year-old Christine, who died when a rock ledge in the mountains crumbled under her feet. And perhaps worst of all, there was Bryan, who despite his devout Christianity finally caved in to his demons and shot himself in the head.

One by one, people I loved and counted on kept dying: Father Bernard, my mother, my dear friend Margaret Joy. Uncles, aunts, in-laws—all washed away with the tide. And it wasn't just the people themselves who kept disappearing; it was big chunks of my own history. I began to hear a faint whooshing sound. I realized it was the sound of my own life speeding by. The situation is summed up in Psalm 103: "Our days are like the grass; like flowers of the field we blossom. The wind sweeps over us and we are gone; our place knows us no more" (103:15–16).

CHRISTIANITY'S CONFRONTATION WITH DEATH

Thinking of this gloomy psalm paradoxically makes me smile, albeit wryly. For contrary to what Marx thought of religion—he called it the "opium of the people"—true religion acknowledges the fragility of life and the suffering that ensues when people we love die. True religion affirms the bleakness of having to live under an irreversible death sentence ourselves. And true religion offers us a choice: we can decide that the inevitability of physical death renders life meaningless and all we can do is dig in and make the best of it until it ends—which is what I used to affirm—or we can choose to believe that, despite the inevitable pain, life is somehow mysteriously, profoundly significant. That every breath we breathe reverberates throughout the universe. That our smallest actions matter on the grandest of scales. This conviction, of course, is harder to achieve, especially in the face of grief and loss.

Catholicism, bless it, affirms the second option. As Saint John Paul II says in *Evangelium Vitae*, "Life on earth is not an ultimate but a penultimate reality, a sacred reality entrusted to us and to be brought to perfection in the gift of ourselves to God and to our sisters and brothers."[1] We are created for what the writer Gil Bailie calls "self-dona-tion," for squandering ourselves in love of God and our fellow beings.[2] That is an inherently meaningful thing to be doing, which means that the suffering that sometimes follows—grief, loneliness, lostness—is also inherently meaningful. Our suffering, in other words, does not make a mockery of our choice. On the contrary, it confirms that we are fully alive. And this, in and of itself, is a life-giving thought, one that I wish our friend Bryan had been able to recall in the depths of his despair.

At the core of the Mass is this recognition of our human condition. At the core of the Mass is this confron-tation with death. At the core is our answer to Moses's either-or ultimatum at Moab: "I have set before you life and death, the blessing and the curse. Choose life" (Dt 30:19). To celebrate the Mass in a state of composure and faith is to automatically choose life. And this I believe too, though so often I am not in a state of composure or even fully-on-board faith when I enter the doors of the church. Though as I face this unrelenting string of deaths, I am balking.

THE UNIVERSAL PRAYER

Pat is now at the ambo to lead us in the Universal Prayer. This prayer, says Joseph Jungmann, "was from ancient times regarded as the most excellent prayer, the prayer, simply, of the Church."[3] In it, we pray for the needs of the universal Church, the unsaved world, those who are sick and suffering, and our own parish. We can pray this way because we, too, have a role in the priesthood: we are meant to become vehicles for the actions between Christ within us and the Holy Spirit. Through our prayer, we personally participate in the salvation of the world.[4] While letting ourselves embrace life despite its inevitable losses is a major step along the spiritual path, this prayer on behalf of others takes us to a whole new level. When we pray together for the needs of the world, we are actually taking up arms against the destructive spiritual forces that cause those losses in the first place. In the Universal Prayer, we become true "intercessors."

What does it mean to intercede? Intercessors "stand between" God and those who through unbelief, despair, or simple weakness need help praying. In their single-minded focus, intercessors act as a channel that vastly increases the power of whatever prayer is already going on. In intercessory prayer, we join our own prayers with those of the saints, praying not for ourselves but for others. It's a truly magnificent vision of what might be possible if only we are willing to take up this burden on behalf of the world.

Nowadays, the Universal Prayer provides one of the most meaningful moments in the Mass for me, but that hasn't always been so. I think about the questions that used to get in the way: Doesn't God already know what we need? And isn't he supposed to be all-loving and all-powerful? Why, then, would he need to be "reminded" through our prayers of intercession about what he ought to be doing out there?

Thanks to one of those dear people who died during that long spate of dyings, a little French-Canadian monk called Father Bernard, I found a different way to think about these thorny questions. Father Bernard, though in his mid-seventies by the time we had this conversation, was one of the most childlike people I'd ever met. Yet not only had he lived through the Great Depression and the Second World War, he'd traveled through some of the most poverty-stricken places on the planet. As a priest for nearly fifty years, he'd listened to the anguished confessions of countless souls. Certainly, he was no stranger to evil. Yet regardless of what he knew from firsthand experience about the sufferings of mankind, he took an exuberant delight in life. One evening in the Hermitage chapel as we met to go on our regular evening walk, I asked him just how he managed to do that.

"Jesus," he said promptly.

"Jesus?"

"I take him with me everywhere."

"What do you mean?"

He peered up at me from under his very French beret. "I invite him to come with me. He comes. That is all." He shrugged one of his typical Gallic shrugs and pushed open the chapel door, holding it open for me to pass through. And as it began to swing shut behind us, he muttered, "Come on, Jesus. Let's go."

I began to think more about Jesus—who he was, what he said about himself, what he did. How much time he spent in prayer. I thought in particular about his enigmatic statements to the disciples at the Last Supper: "Whoever has seen me has seen the Father. . . . The words that I speak to you, I do not speak on my own. The Father who dwells in me is doing his works. Believe me that I am in the Father and the Father is in me, or else, believe because of the works themselves. Amen, amen, I say to you whoever believes in me will do the works that I do, and will do greater ones than these" (Jn 14:9–11).

Suddenly, I got it. The God who to me seemed so unknowable was actually visible in Jesus. And, by extension, in me. Suddenly, my whole sense of self began to shift. I'd been grafted in. ("I am the vine, you are the branches" [Jn 15:5].) I'd been made part of the family, and I now had voting rights. ("If you remain in me and my words remain in you, ask for whatever you want and it will be done for you" [Jn 15:7].) And I had a real job to do—not make-work but incredibly important, even transformative. I was now on the team—the "God-Squad" as another monk, Father Michael Fish, fondly refers to it. My actions, my prayers, were all efficacious, whether or not I ever saw the outcome of any of it. For as Jesus put it, "By this is my Father glorified, that you bear much fruit and become my disciples" (Jn 15:8). In other words, my prayers on behalf of the world were the very thing that helped turn the eyes of God's creatures toward him and hence toward redemption and transformation.

Amazing.

After a brief opening prayer by Father Ken, Pat begins reading the petitions of the day out loud—for Pope Francis, that he might grow in wisdom and love; for peace in the Middle East; for all those who serve in the Armed Forces; for the recent victims of a hurricane. She ends each with "We pray to the Lord," and we respond with "Lord, hear our prayer." Then she moves to the sometimes tricky names on the list of parish sick and dying—Filipino and Spanish and Japanese and Portuguese and Italian names—and for those who have recently died and for the repose of the soul of the particular person for whom this Mass is being said. And over and over, we answer, "Lord hear our prayer."

We are never alone when we are praying. Sometimes I need to be reminded of this. Jesus and the Holy Spirit dwell within me, which means that God the Father dwells in me too. As Jesus assures his disciples—and by extension, all of us at this Mass who are praying the Universal Prayer—"In a little while the world will no longer see me, but you will see me, because I live and you will live. On that day you will realize that I am in my Father and you are in me and I in you" (Jn 14:19–20). And, "Whoever loves me will keep my words, and my Father will love him, and we will come to him and make our dwelling with him" (Jn 14:23).

Amen. May it ever be so.

PART II

The Sacrament

Introduction

I was thirty-four, my first Mass still some years in the future. I was finally back in college to finish my degree, and sitting through my first upper-division English class in more than a decade. Our professor looked like a coach, talked like a coach, and dressed like a coach, but he treated literature with a deferential reverence, as if it were holy writ. He'd memorized more than three thousand lines of poetry, and while he lectured, he thumped back and forth, pulling out quotations at will. I was intimidated by the blazing force of his devotion to the Great Books, but at the same time, I was determined to succeed in this class despite my self-doubt. So I was learning to hold him at bay—to listen attentively without letting myself get swept up in his enthusiasm.

One afternoon he went to the podium and leaned out over the top, raking his gaze across the room as if to gauge our reaction to what was coming next. Then, in his gravelly coach's voice, he began:

> There was a time when meadow, grove, and stream,
> The earth, and every common sight,
> > To me did seem
> > Apparelled in celestial light,

The glory and the freshness of a dream.
It is not now as it hath been of yore;—
   Turn whereso'er I may,
     By night or day,
The things that I have seen I now can see no more.[1]

By this point, I believed that I'd settled all the big questions about religion. My goal was to do as much good as I could do without pretending that it meant anything enduring. This seemed stark and brave to me, and I admired people—writers, especially—who understood this point of view. The world was simply what it was, an often pleasing but sometimes downright horrifying place. The worst response when life became intolerable, however, was to rush into the arms of fantasy for relief—the classic Christian default move, as far as I was concerned.

Why, then, was this poem making me cry? Because suddenly I realized that my nose was running, my eyes streaming, and my stomach clenching. Hastily, I pulled our heavy literature book from the desk and held it up in front of my face so the professor could not see what a cataclysm he had precipitated with his recitation. Unable to stop, I cried with silent, back-shaking sobs throughout the entire "Ode on Intimations of Immortality," Wordsworth's famous lament for his lost childhood vision.

Though at the time I did not realize what had happened to me, it appears that Wordsworth, not in any way an orthodox Christian when he wrote the poem in the early nineteenth century despite his later return to faith, had triggered a deep sorrow for my own lost worldview. He had reminded me with aching clarity of what

I, too, once saw—not a mere conglomeration of physical facts, but a haunted, speaking beauty. In so doing, he had reawakened with a crash my long-dead religious sensibility. I was not seeking such a reawakening and certainly not expecting one, so the force with which it hit me was destabilizing. But it was only in this new state of vulnerability, when the tightly locked gates of my unbelief had been momentarily breached, that the Hound of Heaven began stalking me in earnest.

OUR LOST SENSE OF MYSTERY

For some time after coming back to faith and then entering the Catholic Church, I wondered what else I'd heard in those lines from Wordsworth. For by then, I had guessed they were more than just a poignant reminder of my own childhood innocence. Gradually I began to see that they were about a universal rather than a personal dilemma. Wordsworth was lamenting the loss of an ancient, wisdom-based way of seeing. He was mourning our culture's disappearing capacity for faith in anything but the scientific view of the material world. It did not matter whether we ourselves were scientists or had the slightest clue about how scientists worked or what they considered to be factually true and why. It was simply that science in and of itself now carried the most weight in our society and had become the gold standard for all other disciplines, including philosophy and religion. If you couldn't prove it in a lab, went the wry saying, then it didn't exist.

This loss of our sense of mystery is a somewhat recent development in the history of the human race. Even the word itself—mystery—did not mean to past generations what it means to us today. A mystery was not something to be solved Sherlock-Holmes style; it referred to invisible realities beyond the physical. The ancient belief was that though we can take in a certain amount of data through our senses, we cannot fully capture all that is there. More, we cannot fully comprehend what we do see. Why? For Christians, this is because, as Father Ken's favorite poet, Gerard Manley Hopkins, puts it, "The world is charged with the grandeur of God," and God and his ways are not ever fully comprehensible to human beings.[2]

SACRAMENTAL MYSTERY

The Greek word *mysterion* translated into Latin becomes *sacramentum* and *mysterium*. All three mean "mystery" of the kind that Hopkins was referring to in the poem "God's Grandeur." The *Catechism* says, "In later usage the term *sacramentum* emphasizes the visible sign of the hidden reality of salvation which was indicated by the term *mysterium*." Not only are the sacraments efficacious signs (they cause to happen the very thing to which they point) but they are also vehicles of grace. The *Catechism* explains that "the seven sacraments are the signs and instruments by which the Holy Spirit spreads the grace of Christ the head throughout the Church which is his Body" (*CCC*, 774).

In other words, a sacrament makes use of created physical matter—water, oil, bread—to both effect and reveal the greater spiritual reality that lies invisibly behind it. Understanding this, I could finally see what it was that nineteenth-century British Romantic poets like Wordsworth were trying to recover: not just an older worldview but a sacramental worldview. During this second half of the Mass, the Liturgy of the Eucharist, we Catholics fully experience what has been otherwise largely lost in our time.

From the beginning, the Church understood that a significant portion of what she was and did would necessarily remain incomprehensible to human beings. She was herself a genuine mystery. Far larger than her buildings and great congregations of people, her first purpose "was to be the sacrament of the inner union of men with God." And because "men's communion with one another is rooted in that union with God, the Church is also the sacrament of the *unity of the human race*" (*CCC*, 775). And so she strove to protect these mysteries from the eyes and ears of those outside the baptized body of believers. Without some serious training and enough time to ponder the ramifications of what they were learning, most people were simply not ready to take in what they saw and heard under her roof. [3]

This role of Church as spiritual gate-keeper insured that until the last half of the twentieth century a Catholic lay person attending the Mass would have been aware of a strong supernatural atmosphere. Thanks to the stained glass, the lit tapers, the incense, the tortured body of Christ on the cross, the statues of saints, the Gregorian chants, the chiming of the sance-bells and the earth-shaking clang of the big bells, the Mass remained steeped in mystery well into the modern era. Every detail, from the elaborate priestly vestments to the solemn processionals to the sustained adoration of the Blessed Sacrament to the many intriguing gestures of the priestly celebrants proclaimed that This Was Holy Ground. And that is exactly what the Church understood her calling to be: the juncture between the mundane and the mystical, the hinge between heaven and earth.

Despite the many changes instituted by the Second Vatican Council of the 1960s, the Church continues to be very much rooted in sacramental mystery. Hence the ban still in place concerning non-Catholic participation in the Eucharist. Where there was once grave concern about would-be members accidentally jumbling together pagan and Christian beliefs, today the Church faces an even more formidable challenge: the vast disconnect between the worldview of the gospels and the worldview of today, with its inbuilt skepticism regarding the supernatural. To help bridge this gap, the Second Vatican Council reinstituted the ancient catechumenate (the RCIA classes Mike and I both attended). During this two-year time of preparation, people who've perhaps never even heard the word *mystery* in its older usage are introduced to a new (but actually very old) way of seeing the world.

As for me and my Wordsworth-inspired breakdown in that long-ago literature class, it was only when I participated in my first Eucharist that I understood the nature of the painful interior lacuna that had triggered all those tears. I'd been longing for something I could not even name, for outside the Church, there was nobody who could name it for me. I'd been longing without knowing it for the Great Sacrament itself; I'd been longing to partake of the Body and Blood of Christ.

And now, as we enter the second half of the Mass, I can feel myself internally preparing for that privilege.

Offering

The Preparation of the Altar, the Presentation of the Gifts, the Blessing of the Bread and Wine, the Prayer over the Offerings

The Universal Prayer has been prayed, and the bread and wine will soon be brought forward. Joe and Bill are heading to the front-row pews carrying the offering baskets, and people are digging around in their purses and pockets for their weekly envelopes. I know that St. Patrick's, whose roster includes members at both ends of the economic spectrum, is a remarkably generous parish, and that makes me feel a little pensive, I guess would be the word. Thoughtful. I'd like to be that generous myself—not so much with my money but with my time and energy. Too often, however, I quietly adopt a self-protective stance. There's something in me that after every good deed needs a good long retreat.

Maybe this is why I am intrigued by people I call "light bearers." I watch Joe, dressed in his usual blue Wranglers and Hawaiian shirt, as he hands off the basket. Sicilian by way of Brooklyn, Joe grew up in Arroyo Grande. The joke around town is that there is nobody in a hundred miles he has not met. Both a smiler and a hugger, he's got a hearth-like effect on people. After years of working in the irrigation department of the local farm supply store, he's acquired pretty much every skill known to man. Should you, for example, accidentally shear off the top of your rain-bird sprinkler while mowing the pasture when your husband is out of town for the next three days, just call Joe. He will arrive within ten minutes, and in the back of his little car will be various tool boxes and plumbing parts and other helpful gadgetry, and soon that thirty-foot geyser in the middle of your field will be but a distant memory.

As Joe and Bill move slowly down the aisles toward our pew, Kathy leads us in the "Prayer of Saint Francis." We are singing, "Make me a channel of your peace, where there is hatred let me bring your love," and I am thinking of our grandson Eli. When he first began coming to Mass with us at the age of two, this part of the service was the moment he waited for. Mike let him take care of the offering envelope through what must have seemed like eternity. Once the basket arrived at our seat, he got to very, very carefully place it on top of the other envelopes. Sometimes it took a good thirty seconds to get it just right. But nobody, least of all Joe, ever came down on him for that.

Now we are in a part of the song that seems directly aimed at me, which is an eerie thing that sometimes happens during Mass: "O Master, grant that I may never seek, so much to be consoled, as to console, to be understood,

as to understand, to be loved, as to love with all my soul."
This is what the light bearers do, I think. It's not that they
never consider themselves—of course they do—but their
basic orientation is outward rather than inward.

I find myself thinking about Sister Eva, one of our
indomitable Irish nuns. During her forty years in Arroyo
Grande, Sister Eva envisioned an umbrella organization
for St. Patrick's that could fund and manage a number
of different ministries: the Pantry, which would provide
groceries from the local food bank to families in need;
the Christmas Basket project, which would assemble and
distribute supplies for four hundred Christmas dinners;
the Giving Tree, which would collect presents for kids
who would otherwise not receive any; and the Emergency
Funds program, which offers cash to people in crisis.

Sister Eva's vision—now called Outreach—came into
being more than two decades ago, but what she created
would have quickly died without the ongoing work of
several hundred volunteers. Within this group, which
includes Mike, Joe is in a class by himself. Rather than sign
up for a certain afternoon, he shows up every single day
to see where he is needed. By now he has mastered all the
roles that Katie, Anita, and Margot, the holy trinity who
replaced Sister Eva when she finally left us, can possibly
toss his way.

THE NEW MUSIC

We are still singing. Though today the "Prayer of Saint
Francis" seems especially suited to what's on my mind,

I know that not everyone is similarly moved by it, or for that matter by any of the other songs in *Breaking Bread*. Where most of the changes in the post–Vatican II liturgy were accepted with surprising swiftness by the majority of Catholics, the new music was another story. Some thought that any sort of hymn-singing bespoke Protestantism. Others objected to the work-song feel of the new hymns, believing that American liturgists had been overly influenced by the early sixties' folk music phenomenon. Others simply longed for Gregorian chant—the reverent medieval music that characterized the pre-Reformation Church. Some congregations were initially so put off by the new music that there is actually a book out there called *Why Catholics Can't Sing*.

However, thanks to Kathy, who has never allowed us to be reticent, I would characterize our singing these days as downright lusty. "Make me a channel of your peace," we sing with all our hearts. "Where there is despair in life, let me bring hope."

When the ushers reach the back of the church, they pour the collection into a single basket and then gather up our food donations for the Pantry, which are left in the narthex each Sunday before Mass. While all this is going on, Peter is slowly heading their way with the processional cross. When everybody is assembled, including the couple that has been asked to bring up the gifts (the bread and the wine that are about to become the Body and the Blood of Christ), Peter makes an about-face toward Father Ken and waits for his signal to proceed.

PREPARATION OF THE ALTAR

Meanwhile, the altar is being prepared. Just as the ambo is the focus during the Liturgy of the Word, the altar takes center stage during the Liturgy of the Eucharist, and there are certain items that need to be in place before the priest can receive the gifts. Today, Raphael is the one who lays out the corporal, which looks like a small linen table cloth. On this he sets the gold *chalice*, a sacred cup into which Father Ken will pour the wine for the Eucharist, and also the *paten*, or sacred plate used to hold the consecrated bread. Beside these he places a linen *purificator*, a napkin-like square used to clean the chalice, along with the *Roman Missal*, which is the book of prayers said at the Mass. When all is ready, Father Ken gives Peter the nod and the group in the back processes toward the altar.

HISTORY OF THE OFFERTORY

Though this offertory procession goes back a long way in the history of the Church, curiously enough, it does not go back to the very beginning. For the first couple of centuries, new Christians were so focused on the spiritual implications of Christ's Crucifixion, Resurrection, and Ascension that the material elements of the Mass—the actual bread and the wine—were of lesser importance in their eyes. More, they wanted to separate their own practices from the physical rituals of the pagans and Jews, who continued to make blood sacrifices. But by the end of the second century, this pattern began to change. A greater threat to nascent Christianity than paganism or strict Judaism was emerging. Gnosticism was beginning to hold a powerful allure for some Christian congregations, who were drawn to its promise of spiritual enlightenment for those who became what were called *adepts*. Gnosticism focused on developing a higher consciousness that would ultimately transcend the physical, and the philosophy was close enough to Christianity to be confusing. As Joseph Jungmann puts it, "The peril then no longer lay in the materialism of heathen sacrificial practices, but in the spiritualism of a doctrine that hovered just on the borderline of Christianity."[1]

In response, the Church began to talk more about the elements of the Eucharist as products of soil and rain and sun, and thus gifts of the Creator, important in their own right and not to be overlooked simply because they come from the earth. Just as significantly, in order for these elements to come into fruition, human beings have to labor long and hard. A loaf of bread or a jar of wine thus represents a cooperative effort between God and man; in a sense, the bread and the wine have both an earthly and a heavenly origin.

In the early days of the Church, what we think of today as "the offering" was a contribution, known in the gospels as *corban*, to the community poor box. But by the third century, communicants were also expected to bring a gift of bread or wine for the altar. There was usually a special table or room in which these offerings were left until it was time for them to be prepared for the Eucharist. Parishioners did not limit themselves to gifts of bread and wine either; in one fourth-century floor mosaic, people are pictured carrying a bird, grapes, and flowers.[2] It was not long before regulations limiting the types of acceptable donations had to be set. Bread and wine were all right; so were wax and candles and oil. All other goods were either distributed to the clergy for their upkeep or given to the poor. Gradually, the charitable gifts for the poor, along with the donated bread and wine, were absorbed into the liturgical celebration itself. The priest received the people's offerings and in turn offered them to God.[3] The offerings themselves had become part of the sacrifice being reenacted on the altar.

In time, especially in the Frankish countries, offertory processionals that included everyone in the church became the norm. This practice was rooted in an image of the great Palm Sunday crowd that lined the streets of Jerusalem to meet Jesus riding in on the foal of an ass. But by the eleventh century, it had become common for people to make offerings of money instead of goods, and the full church processional began dying out.[4] In certain areas, however, the ancient custom lingered on. In the early eighteenth century in Ingolstadt, Germany, for example, hat makers and their wives and servants made a solemn offertory procession on the feast day of their patron saint, Barbara. In the early twentieth century in Swabia, Germany, on "Herd Mass" (the day the cattle were driven out to pasture), the whole congregation, led by the "herd boy," circled the altar.[5] During the same period in some churches in Bavaria's Alpine region, people still gathered for the full offertory processional on special feast days, carrying with them donations of flax and sheaves of wheat.[6]

PRESENTATION OF THE GIFTS

Up front, Father Ken gives Peter a slight nod and the cross begins moving toward the altar with gift bearers and ushers pacing slowly behind it. We are still singing: "It is in pardoning that we are pardoned, in giving of ourselves that we receive." Singing at this point in the Mass marks the offertory processional as a jubilant occasion, a chance for us to give back to both God and the Church.[7] I don't recognize the couple carrying the bread and the wine this morning, but that's not unusual; St. Patrick's has more than two thousand families in its rolls, and there are seven Masses each weekend, including two in Spanish. The more important point is that these gift bearers are representing all of us; they are making this offering in our collective name.

When the group reaches the front, Peter secures the processional cross behind the altar, and Father Ken takes the plate of unconsecrated hosts and the pitcher of wine, murmuring his thanks to the gift bearers, who step back and wait. Bill and Joe place the baskets full of offering envelopes and Pantry donations in front of the altar. Then they all bow and move back to their seats.

There are points during every Mass when I feel swept back through the centuries to the ancient Church, and this is one of them. The word *host*, for example, which comes from the Latin *hostia*, is used to designate a living creature destined for sacrificial slaughter. In the Christian tradition, the ultimate hostia is Christ, of course. The Byzantine liturgy ensures that people make this connection even clearer by calling the soon-to-be-consecrated bread the "Lamb." And that allusion goes all the way back to the time of Moses—about 3,500 years ago by now—and the great Passover story, still commemorated all over the world in the Jewish Seder meal.[8] It was the blood of weak little lambs that protected the enslaved Israelites from God's avenging angel as he swept through the countryside, wreaking havoc among the stubbornly disobedient Egyptians. Thanks to the mark of blood made on every Jewish doorpost, the Israelites survived unscathed and were able to successfully flee the chains and whips of their oppressors. When the priest elevates the host, he is also holding up history.

BLESSING THE BREAD AND WINE

Father Ken pours a drop of water into the wine, praying as he does so that we might come to share in the divinity of Christ who humbled himself to share in our humanity. Tradition has long held that these two elements in the chalice, intermingled without confusion, represent the divine nature of Jesus (the wine) along with his human nature (the water).[9] The gifts are then blessed with words derived from ancient prayers such as the Kiddush that are still used in Jewish Sabbath practices today.[10] We respond with "Blessed be God forever."

Raphael appears at Father Ken's side with a towel folded over one arm, waiter style, and a small pitcher of water. As Father Ken quietly says a prayer of contrition, then another derived from Psalm 51—"Wash me, O Lord, from my iniquity, and cleanse me from my sin"—he holds out his hands while Raphael pours a stream of water over them in a ritual that goes back to the days when people regularly made ablutions before praying.[11] However, at this particular juncture—right before the great Eucharistic Prayer—the act takes on even more weight. As Jungmann puts it, "We find the washing of the hands precisely at the place where the holy circle is entered."[12]

Father Ken asks that "my sacrifice and yours may be acceptable to God, the almighty Father," and we respond with "May the Lord accept the sacrifice at your hands for the praise and glory of his name, for our good and the good of all his holy Church." I used to wonder why we prayed this prayer. Was it possible that God might not want our offerings? But then I remembered that the Bible speaks of several rejected sacrifices, as in the Cain and Abel story in Genesis 4, or when God flat-out tells the Israelite priests in the book of Malachi, "I take no pleasure in you. . . . I will not accept any offering from your hands" (Mal 1:10). Moreover, sometimes we ourselves are not, speaking spiritually, in the right place to approach the altar. As Paul reminds us in Romans 12:1, we are to present our "bodies as a living sacrifice, holy and pleasing to God."[13] And for any number of reasons, that's not always possible for us to do.

THE PRAYER OVER THE OFFERINGS

Now Father Ken is praying over the chalice of still-unconsecrated wine and plate of bread, asking once again that God accept them in the name of our Lord Jesus Christ.

This is a moment of quiet drama, akin to the moment when Moses encountered the burning bush and heard the words, "Remove the sandals from your feet, for the place where you stand is holy ground" (Ex 3:5). I don't think that it is just me who feels a little nervous at this point in the Mass. I think back to Father Bernard and his "Let's go, Jesus!" antidote to my skittishness about actually praying to the Creator of the universe. One reason non-belief was attractive to me, I'm pretty sure, was that it allowed me to sidestep the experience of the *mysterium tremendum*, as theologian Rudolf Otto calls it.[14] I did not like the feeling back then—and still don't—of being overshadowed by something so much larger and more powerful than myself. I would much prefer a warmer and fuzzier God. Yet this plea on the part of the priest before he enters the metaphoric Holy of Holies reiterates the fact that God is still who he is, still the Yahweh of the ancient Hebrews, still the totally incomprehensible "I AM," no matter what his effect is on my personal comfort level.

"Amen," we say. This is hard, but we believe it.

SPIRIT BEARERS

Orthodox Christians employ a beautiful word—*pneumataphore*—to describe the holiest of their elders, those so pure of heart they've become healers and sometimes even miracle workers. The term means "spirit bearer." The closest Catholic equivalent would probably be "saint." Sadly, we often assume that holiness on this level is entirely out of our reach, that we are just ordinary people, nothing special, and certainly not capable of shining the light of Christ into this dark world of ours. Yet then I think of Sister Eva and those many who took up her good work when she left—especially Katie, Margot, and Anita. I gaze at the back of Peggy's head, perpetually smiling Peggy, who has been faithfully caring for her aged and infirm husband for years, and I glance toward Mike and Joyce on the side aisle (Eli calls these two, who were his teachers for three years in the local Montessori school, "Mikey" and "Joycie"). They don't have their grandson David with them today—he's recovering from yet another surgery—and their row looks incomplete without him.

I think of Joe and the sheared-off rain-bird sprinkler (yes, it was me) and the way he appeared so promptly and so willingly with his bag of sprinkler-fixing tools—his version of corban. Offering. And how he smiled and gave me a hug and told me I was not a complete dolt after all. And then, how he fixed the mess I'd made. And how that seemed to fill him up instead of deplete him, as these kinds of gestures too often deplete me. In his own humble way, Joe carries more than his bag of tools through life; he also manages to bear the spirit with him wherever he goes. And I would love to know how to do that too. But I am starting to get that this is the work of a lifetime, not something we learn from a book but something we grow into through the daily practice of our faith.

So what, I wonder, is holding me back?

Praising

The Sursum Corda, the Preface, the Sanctus

We have now entered into the heart of the Mass. Everything is slowing down. There's a charged, anticipatory feeling in the air. Like the statue of the Risen Christ that hangs behind him on the front wall, Father Ken extends his hands out toward us. "The Lord be with you," he says.

We open our hands toward him. "And with your spirit," we respond.

I'm not sure why this line affects me so deeply, but it always does. Up until a few years ago, we put it differently. "And also with you," we'd reply, which seemed a perfectly appropriate response. But at times, I'd find myself saying the words almost by rote, as if the priest had just asked me how I was and I'd answered, without thinking, "Fine, thanks. How about you?" Not so with this current retranslation from the Latin, which actually goes back to the earliest days of the Church. The word *spirit* reminds me that when I am in Mass, I'm in a different realm. It reminds me that Father Ken was ordained in the ancient gospel way, through the laying on of hands and the imparting of the Holy Spirit, and that his role as priest is to use the charismatic gifts he received during ordination to fulfill his prophetic function in the Church. Unlike "I'm fine, thanks, how are you?" we only use the expression "and with your spirit" with a priest or deacon, someone who's been ordained in the long apostolic succession originating with Peter.[1]

THE SURSUM CORDA

"Lift up your hearts," says Father Ken, raising his hands. In the days before Vatican II, the beautiful and sonorous Latin words for this mysterious command would have been *sursum corda*. Saint Cyril explains, "It is as if the priest instructs us at this hour to dismiss all physical cares and domestic anxieties, and to have our hearts in heaven with the benevolent God."[2] But the truth is I don't know exactly what "lift up your hearts" means—only whether or not I have done it, because if I have, I am often flooded with a warm, liquid love and an overwhelming sense of surety that this staggering world can be redeemed no matter how dire it all looks at the moment.

Our own palms cupped and raised heavenward, we reply, "We lift them up to the Lord."

"Let us give thanks to the Lord our God," he says.

And we respond with one of the more curious phrases of the Mass, "It is right and just." Despite the juridical-sounding language, we intuitively understand what we are asserting here, for it is actually very simple: in light of all that we have received from God, giving thanks is merely offering to God what is due him, and since justice is defined as giving a person what he is owed, through our thanksgiving we engage in a just act.

Though by now the rest of us have dropped our arms, Peggy is still looking skyward, her cupped hands raised. I've seen this gesture depicted in church mosaics in Italy. It is the ancient posture of *orans*, or prayer, and suddenly I am filled with gratitude toward her for reminding me, week after week, who we are: creatures made in the *imago dei*, the image of God, custom-designed for this very form of worship.

Even after more than twenty years as a Catholic, this realization never fails to stun me.

THE MASS FROM THE EARLIEST DAYS OF THE CHURCH

These days, I cannot imagine any more biblical form of worship than the Mass. Yet growing up, I had the impression that it had been invented by the Catholics at some point shortly before Martin Luther nailed his Ninety-Five Theses to the Wittenberg Castle church door in 1517. I'm not sure where I came up with that notion—certainly not from our pastors and definitely not from the Confirmation classes I attended between the ages of twelve and fourteen. It was simply in the air I breathed, this idea that Catholics had created most of their strange, semi-magical rituals out of whole cloth. Under this view, the Reformation, somewhat accidentally triggered by our very own Martin Luther, represented a return to "pure Christianity."

Years later, during my RCIA training to become a Catholic, I was surprised to discover that a version of the Mass was the primary form of Christian worship from the earliest days of the Church. For the first two centuries, the sacred meal generally took place in private homes rather than in actual churches because it was difficult for the nascent sect to own buildings when Christianity was not yet legal.[3] And thanks to the deadly persecutions going on at the time, it was often too dangerous to meet in a public place anyway. Yet despite all the obstacles, the new religion continued to grow and spread at a rate of 40 percent per decade, and by the middle of the fourth century, soon after it was finally made legal by the Emperor Constantine in the year AD 313, Christians accounted for more than half of the sixty million people living in the Roman Empire.[4]

But even in the beginning, when numbers were still miniscule and believers risked execution at the hands of the state, the Mass—which early on involved proscribed ways of praying and sacramental worship, not simply groups of like-minded friends meeting for a meal—was already taking shape. In the Acts of the Apostles, the history of the infant church from its spectacular beginnings during Pentecost to the imprisonment of Paul in Rome, Luke paints a vivid picture of the new Christian community that referred to itself as The Way: "They devoted themselves to the teaching of the apostles and to the communal life, to the breaking of the bread and to the prayers. Awe came upon everyone, and many wonders and signs were done through the apostles" (Acts 2:42–43).

Within two decades after the Pentecost, we find Paul giving instructions to the church at Corinth about the meaning of the Eucharist: "Therefore, my beloved, avoid idolatry. I am speaking as to sensible people; judge for yourselves what I am saying. The cup of blessing that we bless, is it not a participation in the blood of Christ? The bread that we break, is it not a participation in the body of Christ? Because the loaf of bread is one, we, though many, are one body, for we all partake of the one loaf" (1 Cor 10:14–17).

By the next century, the prayers of the sacred meal— many of which were clearly ancient Jewish table bless- ings—had already been recorded by the Church in Antioch in a manual known as the *Didache*. Three chapters from this book appear to have been composed no later than AD 48, which would make them older than all the books in the New Testament.[5] Here we find a proscription, still in place in the Church today, against unbelievers participating in the breaking of the bread or drinking of the cup: "But let no one eat or drink of your Eucharist unless they have been baptized into the name of the Lord."[6]

We also find a first mention of the Eucharist as sacri- fice: "Every Lord's Day gather yourselves together and break bread, and give thanks after having confessed your transgressions, that your sacrifice might be pure. But let no one who is at odds with his fellow come together with you, until they be reconciled, that your sacrifice might not be profaned. For this is that which was spoken by the Lord: 'In every place and time offer to me a pure sacrifice; for I am a great king, says the Lord, and my name is feared among the nations' (see Mal 1:11, 14)."[7]

By the mid-second century, the Mass had become central to Christian practice. Church Father Irenaeus, born about AD 125, believed it represented the doorway to eternal life: "Our bodies, when they receive the Eucharist, are no longer corruptible, but have the hope of the resurrection to eternity."[8]

The philosopher Justin Martyr in the year AD 150 provides our first detailed account of the ceremony Irenaeus is referring to: "After finishing the prayers, we greet each other with a kiss. Then bread and a cup of water and wine mixed are brought to the one presiding over the brethren. He takes it, gives praise and glory to the Father of all in the name of the Son and the Holy Ghost, and gives thanks at length for the gifts we are worthy to receive from Him. When he has finished the prayers and thanksgiving, the whole crowd standing by cries out in agreement: 'Amen.' . . . After the presiding official has said thanks and the people have joined in, the deacons, as they are styled by us, distribute as food for all those present, the bread and the wine-and-water mixed, over which the thanks had been offered, and also set some apart for those not present."[9]

Some clung to the Eucharist at the expense of their lives. The martyrs of Abitina, third-century North Africans who died during one of the great imperial persecutions launched by Diocletian, provide a case in point: "Christians make the Mass and the Mass makes the Christians, and one cannot exist without the other. . . . We cannot live without the Mass."[10] Though at this point the "liturgical prayer texts . . . were still elastic and continually subject to new influences," at the same time, according to Joseph Jungmann, "there was a unified order, a network of still flexible regulations stamped with the authority of custom. . . . The fundamental design of the prayer of thanks—the Eucharist—[was] everywhere the same."[11]

THE PREFACE

Peggy has lowered her hands and closed her eyes, as have the rest of us. It is time for the Preface prayer, which ushers in what Jungmann calls "the Great Prayer of the Church," otherwise known as the Eucharistic Prayer.[12] Preface prayers vary throughout the Church year, depending on the season or feast day, but all of them focus on giving thanks to God for the Incarnation, for the Passion and Crucifixion and Resurrection, for the Ascension and our redemption—in other words, for the key elements in the Christian story. Not only are we recalling the highlights of our salvation history each time a Preface is prayed, we are consciously enveloping these recollections in gratitude. Father Ken begins:

> It is truly right and just, our duty and our salvation,
> always and everywhere to give you thanks,
> Lord, holy Father, almighty and eternal God.
>
> For just as through your beloved Son
> you created the human race,
> So also through him

with great goodness you formed it anew.

And so, it is right that all your creatures serve you,
all the redeemed praise you,
and all your Saints with one heart bless you.
Therefore, we, too, extol you with all the Angels,
as in joyful celebration we acclaim . . .

THE SANCTUS

Here, Father Ken pauses for the triple Sanctus, sung by
all of us:

Holy, Holy, Holy Lord God of hosts.
Heaven and earth are full of your glory.
Hosanna in the highest.
Blessed is he who comes in the name of the Lord.
Hosanna in the highest.

With this chant, which became part of the Mass by the
end of the first century, we are echoing an important Jewish synagogue rite: the recitation of the Kiddush, or rite
of sanctification, which follows the unrolling and reading
of the scriptural scrolls. The Kiddush includes both the
praise of the cherubim as recorded in Ezekiel 3 and the
song of the mighty angels that is described in the vision
of the prophet Isaiah. (See Isaiah 6.)[13] Theologian Louis
Bouyer believes that the use of these "heavenly canticles"
goes straight back to Temple times, and had in fact probably "been a central feature of the offering of the sacrifice of
incense morning and evening of every day."[14] As we sing

the words of the Sanctus, I think of the powerful passage in Isaiah from which they come:

> I saw the Lord seated on a high and lofty throne,
> with the train of his garment filling the temple.
> Seraphim were stationed above; each of them
> had six wings: with two they covered their
> faces, with two they covered their feet, and with
> two they hovered.
>
> One cried out to the other:
>
> "Holy, holy, holy is the LORD of hosts!
>
> All the earth is filled with his glory!"
>
> At the sound of that cry, the frame of the door
> shook and the house was filled with smoke.
>
> Then I said, "Woe is me, I am doomed! For I
> am a man of unclean lips, living among a people
> of unclean lips, and my eyes have seen the King,
> the LORD of hosts!" Then one of the seraphim flew
> to me, holding an ember which he had taken with
> tongs from the altar.
>
> He touched my mouth with it. "See," he said,
> "now that this has touched your lips, your wick-
> edness is removed, your sin purged."
>
> Then I heard the voice of the Lord saying,
> "Whom shall I send? Who will go for us?" "Here
> I am," I said; "send me!"
>
> (Is 6:1–8)

This verse has always shaken me, and the reminder of God's penetrating question—whom shall I send?—stirs me again today. For too many months I have been a poor candidate for sending, should God come up with a job for me. Prolonged grieving, I am finding, is like being ill without being sick. It saps your energy and your hope. Bitterness is an ever-present temptation.

Ashamed, I lower my head. I've known bitter people, and I don't want to become one. I want to be like Joe. I want to be like Mikey and Joycie, like brave Pat, like Father Bernard and joyful Father Ken. I want the Mass to reshape me the way it seems to so clearly have reshaped them. But there's something getting in the way of that, something I've got to let go of, and how do I do that when I'm not even sure what it is?

Sursum corda, I tell myself. Lift up your heart.

Kneeling

The Eucharistic Prayer, the Epiclesis, the Institution Narrative and Consecration, the Mystery of Faith, the Memorial Acclamation

Having sung "Holy, holy, holy" along with the seraphim, we pull down the wooden kneelers hooked to the back of the pew in front of us and fall to our knees. Here, in this ancient posture of humility and reverence, we will stay until the Great Amen that concludes the ritual of Consecration. First, however, Father Ken will continue the theme of thanksgiving and sacrifice established in the Preface through his recitation of the Eucharistic Prayer. This Great Prayer of the Church, in Jungmann's phrase, has served as the linguistic container for the sacrament of the Eucharist since earliest times. Chapter 9 of the *Didache*, the oldest Christian text outside scripture that we know about, records a version of the prayer that appears to have been in use by the middle of the first century.[1] Today, four different forms of the Eucharistic Prayer are available for use, depending on the season. Characterized by their solemn gravitas, their hint of ancient Roman rhetoric, they prepare us spiritually for what is about to unfold. Because when a priest resumes the Eucharistic Prayer after the profound interruption of the Triple Sanctus, he has moved very near what Jungmann calls "the grace-laden mystery."[2]

Now Father Ken begins:

> You are indeed Holy, O Lord,
> and all you have created
> rightly gives you praise,
> for through your Son our Lord Jesus Christ,
> by the power and working of the Holy Spirit,
> you give life to all things and make them holy,
> and you never cease to gather a people to yourself,
> so that from the rising of the sun to its setting
> a pure sacrifice may be offered to your name.

My hands are folded, my head is bowed, my eyes are closed. I have entered another world, one in which all that lives and moves and breathes has come into existence not through chance but by intention. Me, too. I am included on this list of things God has given life to. I am one of the creatures God has made holy. I wish I could keep this in mind when I am not in Mass. To think of myself as a random product of sperm and egg or chemically driven neurological soup, as my doctor friend Cathy insists, is quite different than knowing that I am a Someone, a Person, brought deliberately into being through the Word himself. I am meant to be; I have a purpose.

THE EPICLESIS

Father Ken holds his hands, palms down over the gifts and prays:

> Therefore, O Lord, we humbly implore you:
> by the same Spirit graciously make holy
> these gifts we have brought to you for consecration,
> that they may become the Body and Blood
> *[here, he makes the Sign of the Cross over the bread and*
> *chalice]*
> of your Son our Lord Jesus Christ,
> at whose command we celebrate these mysteries.

This prayer, called the Epiclesis, is an invocation of the Holy Spirit. Father Ken has just asked God to send the Holy Spirit down upon this simple bread made of wheat and this wine made of crushed and fermented grapes in order that they might be miraculously transformed, via the words of Consecration, into the Body and Blood of Christ. How does this part of the two-thousand-year-old Mass, no matter how many times it occurs, qualify as a genuine miracle? Because we know the laws of nature: material objects like bread and wine cannot change themselves into something else through their own volition. And because such a transformation does not fit within the laws of nature, there is nothing in science that can account for an event like this. Only something completely outside nature—something by definition supernatural—could possibly cause such an effect.

The Holy Spirit is a supernatural intervener with a long history of making the impossible-by-the-tenets-of-natural-law actually occur. It was by the power of the Holy

Spirit that a young virgin called Mary was transformed into the *Theotokos*, the mother of God. It was the Holy Spirit in the form of a dove who descended upon Jesus at the River Jordan while he was being baptized. And it was by the same power of the Holy Spirit that tongues of fire came down upon the heads of the disciples at Pentecost, giving them the ability to understand foreign languages. Invoking the Holy Spirit before he pronounces the words of Consecration is not only a reminder of all this but a wise and prudent thing for Father Ken to do. It protects him from the temptation toward pride or, worse, believing himself capable of priestly magic. It reminds him that it is not by his command that the miracle occurs but through the power of God.

THE MYSTICAL BODY OF CHRIST

Everyone in the church is still on his knees except those who cannot physically pull it off, like the gentleman in front of me (a truly gentle man who always grasps my hand in both of his when we pass the peace), who is elderly and infirm and beloved by his wife (she pats his sweatered back every so often throughout the Mass, as though checking on how he is doing), and who must sit at the very edge of the pew with his head resting in his hands. As I kneel so closely behind him, I can smell the soap he bathed with this morning. I don't know their names, these two people who have clearly been married for decades, whose deep love for one another is so public and transparent, but somehow I know them. And this is

typical, I think, in the Catholic Church, which breathes
nary a word about "Christian fellowship" and spends
little time concocting social events with name tags so that
people will make friends. Instead, the Church depends on
the great unifying effect of the Eucharist to instill love in
us for one another. Which it does. I love this gentle man
and his wife. And I will miss him the day I come to Mass
to find that sometime in the preceding week he left this
world and is now abiding in a different realm.

Which is why I am both glad for and believe in the
Catholic doctrine of the Mystical Body of Christ. As the
Catechism puts it, "Believers who respond to God's word
and become members of Christ's Body, become intimately
united with him." This means we are "taken up into communion with him and with one another" (*CCC*, 790). How
does this work itself into our daily lives?

The unity of the Mystical Body produces and stimu-
lates charity among the faithful: "From this it follows that
if one member suffers anything, all members suffer with
him, and if one member is honored, all members together
rejoice." The unity of the Mystical Body also triumphs
over all human divisions: "For as many of you as were
baptized into Christ have put on Christ. There is neither
Jew nor Greek, there is neither slave nor free, there is neither male nor female; for you are all one in Christ Jesus"
(*CCC*, 791).

I know that the reason I always feel more hopeful at
Mass, despite my occasional broodiness, is because of
this visceral connection with these anonymous family
members of mine. For that is what we are, the gentle man

and I: family, whose links transcend the merely biolog-
ical, and whose love for one another transcends death.
Because, as Hebrews 12:1 points out, whenever we gather
for worship, we are surrounded by a "great cloud of witnesses"—that is, with those fellow Christians who have
passed from this earth yet are still alive in Christ, still part
of the Mystical Body.

THE INSTITUTION NARRATIVE AND CONSECRATION

And now Father Ken begins to recite the words of what's
called the Institution Narrative, which are the words Jesus
spoke to his disciples during the Last Supper:

> For on the night he was betrayed
> he himself took bread,
> and, giving you thanks, he said the blessing,
> broke the bread and gave it to his disciples, saying:
> TAKE THIS, ALL OF YOU, AND EAT OF IT,
> FOR THIS IS MY BODY,
> WHICH WILL BE GIVEN UP FOR YOU.

Here, he raises the large unbroken host and, holding it
in both hands, displays it to every section of the church.
Then he lays it back on the paten and makes a genuflection before going on:

> In a similar way, when supper was ended,
> he took the chalice,
> and, giving you thanks, he said the blessing,
> and gave the chalice to his disciples, saying:

TAKE THIS, ALL OF YOU, AND DRINK FROM IT,
FOR THIS IS THE CHALICE OF MY BLOOD,
THE BLOOD OF THE NEW AND ETERNAL COVENANT,
WHICH WILL BE POURED OUT FOR YOU AND FOR MANY
FOR THE FORGIVENESS OF SINS.

DO THIS IN REMEMBRANCE OF ME.

As he did with the host, Father Ken raises the chalice high, again displaying it to everyone in the church, before setting it back on the corporal and making another prolonged genuflection. I think about the words, "Do this in remembrance of me." They sound simple, but what do they really mean? Our normal tendency is to interpret the verb *remember* as designating an act of the will. We throw our minds backward, so to speak, in order to momentarily recall events from the past. Yet these words at the end of the Consecration, referred to as the *anamnesis*, or memorial, are not merely about dutifully recalling what Jesus did; according to the ancient sacramental vision to which we Catholics subscribe, they are making the events of the Last Supper and Crucifixion actually present to us. We are both there and here at the same time.

THE MYSTERY OF FAITH

Father Ken then says something that always makes the back of my neck tingle. It's a simple phrase. But given what has just happened—the miraculous transformation of bread and wine into the Body and Blood of Christ—it is said during an especially charged moment, a moment during which I am aware that there are two miracles going on simultaneously, the second one being my being here at all. He says, "The mystery of faith," and for a moment as he looks out over the congregation, we lock eyes. For he of all people, my former colleague at the university, knows just how amazing it is that I should be kneeling in this church. Given where I started, where I got myself to, and how long it took me to get back, faith is indeed the greatest of mysteries.

Suddenly, I am close to tears. For what a labyrinthine, unlikely path I have been on. After that class on the British Romantics and my soul-shaking experience with Wordsworth's great poem lamenting our lost spiritual vision, I began to think seriously about teaching English at the college level. At forty, I was lecturing at the same university where I'd matriculated. Meanwhile, I continued sitting in on philosophy classes, reading theology, and pondering the great questions. Along the way, I published my first novel, the story of a young pianist trying to sort out her conflicted spiritual longings. Back in those days, it was Father Ken—at that time not a priest but a professor—who became one of the few friends in the department I could talk to about religion. Little did either of us know that someday he would be speaking the words of Consecration at a Mass that included me in the pews.

I think about how lonely I often felt back then—how out of touch with an academic culture that for the most part saw my struggles with faith as foolish and misplaced. Yet as I sit here absorbing these radiant words—the mystery of faith—I can see that the university experience, painful as it sometimes was, helped bring me to this moment. What I learned from those philosophy courses is that some kind of absolute goodness and truth must ground all rational thought or we lose the very notion of thinking. From studying all those great works of literature, I discovered that ungrounded characters are just as vaporous and unsatisfying as ungrounded argument. And from my own fiction writing, I began to see that unless a story pointed to something beyond the sum of its own physical details, it might be entertaining but it would never be great.

I sigh, thinking of what a long process all this has been. And of how grateful I am to be here, listening to my old friend Father Ken speak the words of salvation.

THE MEMORIAL ACCLAMATION

After the *mysterium fidei*, or Father Ken's reminder that faith itself is a mystery, we make our Memorial Acclamation, one of three acclamations made by the whole congregation during the course of the Mass. Though there are several versions available, today we respond with the following:

> We proclaim your Death, O Lord,
> and profess your Resurrection
> until you come again.

I glance at Mike, looking for that wondering baby-chick expression I get such a kick out of, but at this moment of Consecration, his eyes are closed and his face is not giving away a thing. And I think, as I have thought so many times since we married nearly thirty years ago, that there are mysteries almost as deep as the mystery of faith. One of these is the mystery of personhood, and I am confronting it right this moment. How can we work with someone, eat with someone, sleep with someone, and share almost everything on our minds with that very same someone for nigh unto three decades and not know, by osmosis or whatever, everything he is thinking? But we can't. That is both the frustration and the glory of marriage. There is a private part of the self that is not readable, even by the person we love most and sometimes not even by ourselves. Kierkegaard, that lonely Danish Lutheran, believed that faith is housed in this intensely private part of us and cannot be conveyed to others. Our secret relationship with God is ours alone.

I can understand what Kierkegaard meant. Even the marriage of the gentle man in front of me and his loving, sweater-patting wife do not unite them the way one would think. They will never be utterly permeable to each other. But there is a spiritual intimacy available to them that Kierkegaard clearly never experienced. Mike and I are about to commune with this anonymous family of ours in a sacramental experience that is the antithesis of private, individual faith. We are about to become united at the deepest level with people whose race, ethnicity, gender, economic status, education level, occupation, and favorite television shows are completely irrelevant.

We don't even need to know their names.

Assenting

The Intercessions, the Doxology, the Great Amen

The gifts on the altar look exactly as they looked before the words of Consecration. Yet as Catholics, we who kneel during this Mass believe they have been changed into the Body and Blood of Christ. If there is any belief more baffling to those outside the faith—and even, at times, to those inside the fold—I cannot imagine what that might be.

Theologians have worked hard at crafting a philosophical explanation for Jesus' most mysterious and difficult teaching, which baldly states that unless we eat his flesh and drink his blood, we do not have life within us:

> Whoever eats my flesh and drinks my blood has eternal life, and I will raise him on the last day. For my flesh is true food, and my blood is true drink. Whoever eats my flesh and drinks my blood remains in me and I in him. Just as the living Father sent me and I have life because of the Father, so also the one who feeds on me will have life because of me. This is the bread that came down from heaven. Unlike your ancestors who ate and still died, whoever eats this bread will live forever.
> (Jn 6:54–58)

Catholics believe that these words of Jesus are not simply metaphorical, and that when we take wine and bread that has been sacramentally transformed into our own bodies, we ourselves are sacramentally transformed.

TRANSUBSTANTIATION

The technical term for this mystical transformation of the Eucharistic gifts into spiritual food is transubstantiation. The *Catechism* explains that "by the consecration of the bread and wine there takes place a change of the whole substance of the bread into the substance of the body of Christ our Lord and of the whole substance of the wine into the substance of his blood" (*CCC*, 1376). Pope Benedict XVI (writing as Cardinal Joseph Ratzinger) elaborates, "The Lord takes possession of the bread and wine; he lifts them up, as it were, out of the setting of their normal existence into a new order; even if, from a purely physical point of view, they remain the same, they have become profoundly different."[1]

But the word *substance* can still be difficult to grasp, especially when we think of it strictly in terms of what we can touch and measure. In fact, the Church adopted the language of substance—borrowed from Aristotelian philosophy—to help us avoid one of two errors: first, to look upon the elements of the Eucharist only in a physical light (we are eating Christ's actual flesh), and second, to assume that the bread and wine are simply symbolic manifestations of his Body and Blood.[2] Either mistake will effectively block us from experiencing the profound mystery of Holy Communion. As the famous American (and Catholic) writer Flannery O'Connor once put it, "Well, if it's a symbol, to hell with it."[3]

I'm neither theologian nor trained philosopher, so the philosophical language adopted by the Church during medieval times is difficult for me to get my head around, and I've spent years trying to get a rudimentary grasp of it. But as best as I can figure out, in Aristotelian terminology, substance refers to the "thing in itself," its "true being." Yet this reality, this fundamental basis of being, is distinct from its physical properties. Properties like color, size, and shape are what help us tell one thing from another. For example, purple-ness, tartness, and musky aroma are properties of wine, and crustiness, yeasty flavor, and the color golden-brown are properties of baked bread.

Not all properties, however, carry equal weight. Aristotle distinguished between properties that are essential (without them, the thing cannot be) and properties that are accidental. Accidental properties (also known as accidents) are characteristic qualities of the thing-in-itself but aren't required for it to be what it is. For example, wine can be wine whether it is made with pinot noir or cabernet grapes, and bread can be bread whether it is made of sour dough or rye. Even more to the point, a Catholic can be a Catholic whether he's Italian, African, Ecuadorean, or bald—according to the logic of Aristotle, his ethnicity and the condition of his hair are accidents that don't change the fact of his Catholicism.

Thus, when the bread and the wine are transubstantiated into the Body and Blood of Christ, their substance changes but their accidents remain the same. Another way to think of this is that their reality changes but their appearance remains what it was. Or as Pope Paul VI puts it, "The bread and wine have ceased to exist after the consecration so that the adorable body and blood of the Lord Jesus from that moment on are really before us under the sacramental species of bread and wine."[4]

CHRIST'S TRANSFIGURED BODY

Even when we accept the theological explanation, it can be difficult to fully grasp what Jesus was talking about. I know it is for me. His own disciples murmured, "This saying is hard; who can accept it?" Jesus responded, "Does this shock you? What if you were to see the Son of Man ascending to where he was before?" (Jn 6:61–62).

When we are struggling to get our heads around the doctrine of transubstantiation, it's important to remember that Jesus received a new kind of body after death—one that was not immediately recognizable even to the disciples who had been closest to him, one that could pass through locked doors but still retained the marks of the nails. Even before the Crucifixion, this transformed body was momentarily revealed to Peter, James, and John during the Transfiguration: "His face shown like the sun and his clothes became white as light" (Mt 17:2). When Moses and Elijah appeared, each of whom had been dead for hundreds of years, their transformed bodies were equally radiant and light filled.

So we can rest assured that when we eat his Body and drink his Blood, we are not eating his earthly flesh. We are not cannibals. As Jesus points out, "It is the spirit that gives life, while the flesh is of no avail" (Jn 6:63).When we consume the Eucharistic elements, we are partaking of the divine substance, for as it says in the Creed, Jesus is "consubstantial with the Father." This spiritual food he continually offers us through the Eucharist, like the manna that fell each night in the desert so that Moses and the Israelites would not die of starvation, is that which allows us to participate in the divine life. The Eucharist is how we sustain and nourish the mysterious relationship Jesus describes in his last discourse: "I am in my Father and you are in me and I in you" (Jn 14:20).

And this is about all we can say, the limit of human comprehension when it comes to the mystery of the Eucharist. Because what we are really banking on is not the correct philosophical explanation but the fact that Jesus told us to do what we are about to do. And we trust him and seek to obey him, no matter how difficult it is to understand what's happening here.

BAKING BREAD AND MAKING WINE

I have to admit that for me, the term "transubstantiation" only comes to life when I think about real bread and real wine and how they get made. I have no clue where I first found the oatmeal, flaxseed meal, almond meal recipe I use for my weekly bread baking (probably *Mother Earth*

News). But "grandma toast" has long been a staple in our family. And it is a process.

First, I fill a cereal bowl with warm water, add a teaspoon of sugar, and shake in some yeast. Our grandkids are fascinated by the smelly yeast, which they know is alive and will make the loaves rise. Then I pour the oats and other meals, plus a little salt, into my big blue-striped, cream-colored crockery bowl, stir them together with a wooden spoon, and add plenty of honey, oil, and boiling water. By the time the yeast is threatening to overflow the cereal bowl, the grains are cool enough for me to mix everything together. Then comes the flour, cups of it, and the first kneading and first rising, all of which can take more than an hour. After repeating the process for the second time, I shove the doughy loaves into my ancient Wolf oven, and forty-five minutes later, the transformation from dry yeast and raw grains now complete, the grandkids are happily consuming big slabs of hot, crusty, and incredibly fragrant grandma toast.

The parables of Jesus often mention bread ("The kingdom of heaven is like yeast that a woman took and mixed with three measures of wheat flour until the whole batch was leavened" [Mt 13:33]). Some of his most spectacular miracles also involve bread: the feeding of the five thousand with five loaves and two fish, for example. But wine is also high on the list when it comes to parables and miracles. Not only does Jesus change vats of water into good wine at the wedding at Cana, he uses wine as a metaphor for faith, saying that you can't pour the new stuff into old wineskins or they will burst.

Even though we store our homemade merlot, barbera, and petite sirah in recycled bottles instead of goat skins, I get what he is talking about. Every fall Mike and his buddies pick several tons of grapes at one local vineyard or another, then dump them inside big vats in Floyd and Carolyn's barn, adding just the right amount of yeast per pound and stirring the whole sludgy mass daily until the sugar content hits zero. This is the signal that the mixture has turned to alcohol and the guys can put it through the crusher and into the barrels. There it sits for a whole year, with Floyd tending it like a mother until it is ready to be bottled, which we do in an all-day event that includes a spectacular potluck and plenty of former grapes.

Knowing firsthand how much hard human labor goes into the production of bread and wine, I am not at all surprised that Jesus chose them as the elements of the Eucharist. They may have been common fare in his day, but given how much time and energy they took to make, they were also highly valued. Both start with a seed (wheat) or a cutting (grapes). Both require watering, weeding, and harvesting. Grapevines also need careful pruning. Before the basic ingredients can even be put to use, they must survive wind and storms, rats and insects, the beating of the sun. That they do survive is another kind of miracle.

"Every year," says C. S. Lewis, "as part of the Natural order, God makes wine. He does so by creating a vegetable organism that can turn water, soil, and sunlight into a juice which will, under proper conditions, become wine. Thus, in a certain sense, He constantly turns water into wine, for wine, like all drinks, is but water modified."[5]

Though Lewis is not talking about transubstantiation here but instead the kind of mundane "miracle" we tend to take for granted—the transformation of tiny seeds into fruit-bearing plants—his point is well taken. Even in the natural world, God is constantly working his works. Recalling this fact helps me get my mind around the far greater mystery of matter being transformed into that which is entirely spiritual.

THE INTERCESSIONS

Father Ken, still standing before the consecrated gifts, now completes the great Eucharistic Prayer, this time asking that we might "obtain an inheritance" with the saints who have gone before us:

> Therefore, O Lord, as we celebrate the memorial
> of the saving Passion of your Son,
> his wondrous Resurrection
> and Ascension into heaven,
> and as we look forward to his second coming,
> we offer you in thanksgiving
> this holy and living sacrifice.
>
> Look, we pray, upon the oblation of your Church
> and, recognizing the sacrificial Victim by whose death
> you willed to reconcile us to yourself,
> grant that we, who are nourished
> by the Body and Blood of your Son
> and filled with his Holy Spirit,
> may become one body, one spirit in Christ.

May he make of us
an eternal offering to you,
so that we may obtain an inheritance with your elect,
especially with the most Blessed Virgin Mary, Mother
    of God,
with your blessed Apostles and glorious Martyrs
and with all the Saints,
on whose constant intercession in your presence
we rely for unfailing help.

May this Sacrifice of our reconciliation,
we pray, O Lord, advance the peace and salvation of
    all the world.
Be pleased to confirm in faith and charity
your pilgrim Church on earth,
with your servant Francis our Pope and Richard our
    Bishop,
the Order of Bishops, all the clergy,
and the entire people you have gained for your own.

Listen graciously to the prayers of this family,
whom you have summoned before you:
in your compassion, O merciful Father,
gather to yourself all your children
scattered throughout the world.
To our departed brothers and sisters
and to all who were pleasing to you
at their passing from this life,
give kind admittance to your kingdom.
There we hope to enjoy for ever the fullness of your
    glory
through Christ our Lord,
through whom you bestow on the world all that is good.

This morning I am struck by many phrases—"the holy and living sacrifice" we are about to offer; the request that we may become "one body, one spirit in Christ"; the saints "on whose constant intercession" we rely for help. Until I became a Catholic, it never crossed my mind that those who have died before us are still alive, loving us and praying for us. But the phrase that really arrests me this morning is "your pilgrim Church on earth." I have been a pilgrim myself—a solo round-the-world trip years ago—so I know what it is like to be on the road, gingerly picking your way through troubles you never anticipated, craving the security of home, knowing you've got to keep going. A real pilgrimage strips you of your identity. You are a stranger among strangers, dependent on the good-will of others. You are vulnerable. You can easily become a magnet for evil. But at the same time, you are full of hope. For up ahead, barely discernible through the alien mists, is what you are seeking. You are arriving, but not yet. So you teeter on the knife edge between presumption and despair, your hand in God's. As Jesus put it, "Foxes have dens and birds of the sky have nests, but the Son of Man has nowhere to rest his head," (Mt 8:20) and when you are a pilgrim, you see just what he meant.

Yet when you are Catholic, you are never alone on this pilgrimage. This section of the Eucharistic Prayer acknowledges that we are celebrating this Mass in union with the whole Church, including those who lived two millennia ago, those who live thousands of miles away from us, and those who speak languages we've never heard spoken out loud before. It says we are praying with and for all these fellow believers, along with our pope, our local bishop, and the great council of bishops, not to mention the saints, the apostles, and the Virgin Mary. We are not lonely pilgrims on the road; we live and move and have our being amidst a veritable cloud of witnesses.

THE DOXOLOGY

Now Father Ken is raising both the chalice and the host and is singing in his resonant tenor the closing *doxology*, or hymn of praise, of the Eucharistic Prayer. It takes the form of a second Epiclesis, or invocation of the Holy Spirit:

> Through him, and with him, and in him,
> O God, almighty Father,
> in the unity of the Holy Spirit,
> all glory and honor is yours,
> for ever and ever.

The phrase "through him" echoes the prologue of the Gospel of John, which says of Christ: "In the beginning was the Word, and the Word was with God and the Word was God. He was in the beginning with God. All things came to be through him, and without him nothing came to be. What came to be through him was life, and this life was the light of the human race: the light shines in the darkness, and the darkness has not overcome it" (Jn 1:1–5).

The phrase "all glory and honor" comes out of the book of Revelation, with its description of the last great "Mass of the world" at the close of the age. In this brief doxology right before we partake of the Body and Blood of Christ, in other words, we are reminded of both the Alpha and the Omega, both the creation of the universe and its final end.

THE GREAT AMEN

We have by now been kneeling for some time, but this is our signal to rise as we simultaneously sing the Great Amen, which is the word *amen* repeated several times and which signals our assent, as the congregation of St. Patrick's, to everything that has occurred up to this moment. The Great Amen is truly ancient; Justin Martyr records that in the second century, "All the people present joyfully acclaim: 'Amen,'" and the third-century Dionysius of Alexandria describes the Mass thusly: "He has listened to the Eucharistic prayer, he has answered 'Amen' with the others, he has approached the altar and stretched out his hand to receive the sacred food."[6] With our own "amen," we join centuries of Catholics in preparation for Holy Communion.

As I rise to my feet, singing, I realize something about that still-tender, still-wounded place inside my heart: It's that some of those lost beloveds of mine never experienced this moment. Never gave their assent. I wonder about my grandchildren. How will their faith develop or not develop? What will cause them to embrace it or let it go? But much as I'd love to know how the future will unfold for them, I can't. For they are not just little people but little persons, which makes them mysteries beyond a grandmother's ken.

Praying

The Lord's Prayer,
the Passing of the Peace

For a moment, I am proud of myself for recognizing my limits, but then I have to smile. I know Mike would smile if he could hear what I was thinking. Because I'm still (and probably always will be) learning the art of renouncing undue worry. "Undue" in the sense that there's nothing I can do about whatever it is I'm worrying about, so why spend entire sleepless nights wringing my hands in frustration and dread over what can't be changed except by God?

I became an *oblate,* or lay member, of New Camaldoli Hermitage in 1999 in part because I was tired of being buffeted by my worries. I did not know if it were even possible, but I longed for a more focused (read: anxiety-free) heart and mind. As a would-be oblate, I spent several years reading and consulting with a spiritual director and the oblate chaplain to see whether or not I understood what the choice would entail. Then I made some brief but life-changing vows in front of the assembled community before going back to my normal life in a different way. For a long time being an oblate-in-the-world proved discouragingly difficult but slowly I began to get the hang of it. The key to peace seemed to lie in relinquishing my tight-fisted control over life.

When I attended my first Mass so many years ago—more than a decade before I became an oblate—what attracted me so strongly, I now believe, was not so much the intriguing plethora of beautiful liturgical phrases and melodies, nor was it the haunting gestures of crossing and genuflecting and kneeling, nor even the lit tapers and stained glass and gold chalice and golden cups, though all of this was new to me and striking. Instead, it was the utter simplicity and peace at the heart of all that pageantry: it was the Eucharist—so much contained in so little. As Sofia Cavalletti describes it, "In the Eucharist, not only are the worlds of God and the human person united, but also, through us and Christ's mediation, the whole subhuman world is united to the world of God. The Eucharist has infinite scope and repercussions in history and in the farthest ranges of the created world: It reaches the very summit of the world."[1]

Though my oblate vow has provided an anchor for me, what has focused my life in the long run is the ongoing experience of the Eucharist. It has become a refuge of safety and peace like no other. As for my old nemesis, "undue worry," I am convinced that it will never be fully conquered. But at least I am no longer worrying about my worry problem, and that's progress for sure.

THE LORD'S PRAYER

Having made our assent—the Great Amen—we are back on our feet and already reaching for one another's hands as Father Ken invites us to join him in the Lord's Prayer. Sometimes we sing this, sometimes we don't, but always our hands are linked, the entire congregation physically joined. Not all Catholic congregations join hands for the Lord's Prayer this way—in some parishes, in fact, this practice is a controversial one. Yet historically, the Lord's Prayer has demanded special rituals. In some ancient churches, people prostrated themselves on the floor as a sign of reverence for the prayer Jesus himself taught the disciples; here at St. Patrick's, we hold on to one another like children as we directly address our Creator using words that are "truly the summary of the whole gospel," as Tertullian puts it.[2] Maybe this is why early Christian communities prayed this prayer three times a day (*CCC*, 2767). Saint Thomas Aquinas calls it "the most perfect of prayers" because "this prayer not only teaches us to ask for things, but also in what order we should desire them" (quoted in *CCC*, 2763).

Standing upright before God, hands joined, heads bowed, eyes closed, we begin:

> Our Father, who art in heaven,
> hallowed be thy name;
> thy kingdom come,
> thy will be done
> on earth as it is in heaven.

Though I have prayed this prayer thousands of times, I am always struck anew by the weightiness of each word as it comes off my tongue. The name "Father," for example: I know that even the Chosen People did not dare address God this way, for that would have been presumptuous, possibly blasphemous. Yet Jesus tells his disciples that not only may they approach God with this name on their lips, they are even allowed to use the term *Abba*, which is an Aramaic word that signifies filial intimacy (Rom 8:16). For now that they have seen him, Jesus tells them, they have seen the Father (Jn 14:9). *Abba* reminds me of the childish name we siblings continued to call our gentle father well into our adult years: Daddy, who died too young.

The word *our* makes me think of Bill and Lynnette and Joe and Cindy, of Pat and Larry and Mikey and Joycie, of Father Ken and Kathy and Raphael and the gentle, name- less man in front of me; it reminds me that my primary relationship to the world is not private but communal. It conjures up the Body of Christ, the Communion of Saints, the cloud of witnesses by whom, as the years run swiftly by, I am increasingly aware I am surrounded: that great cloud of invisible and beneficent presences.

The phrase "who art in heaven" brings back Lutheran Sunday school and the day that we realized Pastor Art's son had gotten it all wrong. "Our Father," we overheard him earnestly praying, "who is Art, in heaven." As for the word *heaven*, I realize in this moment that I have never been comfortable with the term, associating it with a certain kind of near-death experience literature that has always seemed sensationalist to me. And maybe I am also harkening back to the days when I used to snicker at the notion of a mythological "sky god" who rules from the clouds. But I know what Saint Augustine has to say about this matter: we are not talking about sky gods at all; this phrase is "rightly understood to mean that God is in the hearts of the just, as in his holy temple." It also means that "the ones who pray"—and I am included in this group—"should desire the one they invoke to dwell in them" (quoted in *CCC*, 2794).

Poor Candy, whose right hand I am clasping in my left, is getting tired of holding her arms up so high. I can feel her starting to droop and lower my own arm to help her out. She's so petite—probably less than five feet tall—and at eighty-something, she's making what amounts to a heroic effort. She gives my hand a squeeze of thanks.

For me, the phrase "hallowed be thy name" seems more than a little dangerous in this era of religion-generated terrorism. Might not we conclude that it's totally up to us to enforce properly reverent behavior? Isn't this how zealots think? But according to the *Catechism*, what I am instead asking is that the holiness of God's name be reflected in the way I live my life (*CCC*, 2807). And 1 John 4:7 tells me how that should be: "Beloved, let us love one another because love is of God; everyone who loves is begotten by God and knows God. Whoever is without love does not know God, for God is love."

As for the coming of the kingdom, I can see that in one sense it has already arrived; I experience it in the Eucharist. In another, however, this cry is for the end of times when the old world will pass away and a new heaven

and a new earth will be born. The will of God is that all
shall be part of this kingdom, and so when I ask that his
will be done, I am in essence praying for the redemption
of the whole universe.

> Give us this day our daily bread,
> and forgive us our trespasses,
> as we forgive those who trespass against us.

I sneak a look around me at all the raised arms and
lowered heads of my fellow parishioners. Though some
of us are wealthy and some of us are poor, none of us,
I am guessing, live like the farmers and fishermen of
Jesus' day. Thus, the simple request that God provide me
physically with what I need to survive cannot possibly
strike me, who have so much, in the way it must have
affected Jesus' followers. But this is the most basic plea
a person can make: *Do not forget me, God. Do not forget to
send the rain and the sun. Do not let me or any of the people
I love go hungry.* In a deeper sense, it is also a confession
of spiritual hunger: *Send me manna, Lord. Feed me in the
Eucharist.* Asking God to forgive my trespasses assumes
that, believer or not, I will continue to sin, sometimes in
obvious ways and sometimes so secretly that even I don't
know what I've done. When I go to Confession, I almost
always have to wrack my brains for a bit. It's easy to think
that because I am trying to be good, I actually am good,
in which case, what do I need to confess? This morning,
however, I know—I need to confess my same old sin of
desperately clinging to the control knobs.

Tough as it is to think about my constant need for forgiveness, however, the next line of the prayer—"as we forgive those who trespass against us"—is the real kicker. I am asking God to forgive me in the same way I forgive others? I open my eyes again and boldly stare at Mike. Clearly, I am doomed. Yet the link between these phrases makes sense: Jesus firmly states the relationship between them. "If you forgive others their transgressions, your heavenly Father will forgive you. But if you do not forgive others, neither will your Father forgive your transgressions" (Mt 6:14–15). The *Catechism* explains why God's forgiveness and our own must go hand-in-hand: when we refuse to forgive our brothers and sisters, "our hearts are closed and their hardness makes them impervious to the Father's merciful love" (*CCC*, 2840).

> And lead us not into temptation,
> but deliver us from evil.

Back in my Sunday school days I was baffled by why I needed to ask God not to lead me into temptation. It just didn't make sense. And actually, it doesn't make sense. I have since discovered that the problem is one of translation. It's impossible to convey the Greek verb used in scripture in a single English word. The closest interpretation is something like this: "Do not allow us to enter into temptation," coupled with "do not let us yield to temptation" (quoted in *CCC*, 2846). Keep us away from it, and if we do get into it, don't let us succumb.

We stop, and Father Ken adds what is known as the Embolism of the Lord's Prayer—truly, some of the most beautiful words we hear during the Mass:

> Deliver us, Lord, we pray, from every evil,
> graciously grant peace in our days,
> that, by the help of your mercy,
> we may be always free from sin
> and safe from all distress,
> as we await the blessed hope
> and the coming of our Savior, Jesus Christ.

If only it were that easy—that God would just whisk away the worry without me having to work so hard and unsuccessfully at giving it up. But recently I've been realizing—maybe as one of the positive side effects of helping those beloveds of mine die—that occasional anxiety is part and parcel of being human. It's a natural stirring up of the psyche that occurs when we are facing something new. It could even mean we are growing. But only, of course, if we can keep ourselves from slipping into the control-freak mode.

> For the kingdom,
> the power and the glory are yours
> now and forever.

THE PASSING OF THE PEACE

Mike and I are still holding hands as the Lord's Prayer comes to a close. We often do that—hold each other's hands—as we wait for the "passing of the peace" to begin.

If Eli and Sophie were with us right now, they would still be coming back to life after the homily, which for them, at the ages of three and barely seven, is the most trying portion of the Mass and through which they mostly stare dazedly at the back of the pew in front of them. They like holding hands during the Lord's Prayer, however, especially because it is the precursor to their favorite moment all morning—the passing of the peace.

This is another ancient custom in the Church. Saint Paul says, "Greet all the brothers with a holy kiss" (1 Thes 5:26). He repeats this in Corinthians and Romans: "Greet one another with a holy kiss" (1 Cor 16:20, 2 Cor 13:12, Rom 16:16). The custom was still alive by the time of Saint Gregory the Great, who recounts in his *Dialogues* the story of some monks about to go down with a sinking ship. Each of them, he says, gave the other the kiss of peace, then partook of the Eucharist together.[3] The fifth-century Apostolic Constitutions state: "Let the bishop salute the church and say, 'The peace of God be with you.' And let the people answer, 'And with thy spirit' and let the deacon say to all, 'Salute one another with the holy kiss.' And let the clergy salute the bishops, the men of the laity salute the men, and the women salute the women."[4]

This way of passing the peace was easily managed as women and men usually sat on opposite sides of the sanctuary. However, there were concerns that this intimate gesture could become risky, or at the very least, unseemly, as congregations grew larger. So the English added a new twist in the thirteenth century with the introduction of an ornamented plaque known as the *pax-brede* or *pax-board* that could be kissed and then handed on from altar to laity.[5]

Today, at least in America, we generally shake hands during this moment in the Mass as a way of expressing "peace, communion, and charity," in the words of the *Roman Missal*. This gesture is inserted into the Mass right before we commune together and reminds us of Jesus' injunction regarding the state of our heart prior to making our sacrifice: "Therefore, if you bring your gift to the altar, and there recall that your brother has anything against you, leave your gift there at the altar, go first and be reconciled with your brother, and then come and offer your gift" (Mt 5:23–24). At the moment we are about to partake of the Body and Blood of Christ together—the great sacrament of unity—it is critical that we are able to look upon one another with no dark and vengeful shadows blocking our vision.

Father Ken prays:

> Lord Jesus Christ,
> who said to your Apostles:
> Peace I leave you, my peace I give you,
> look not on our sins,
> but on the faith of your Church,
> and graciously grant her peace and unity
> in accordance with your will.
> Who live and reign for ever and ever.

We say, "Amen."
He says, "The peace of the Lord be with you always."
We respond, "And with your spirit."

He says, "Let us offer each other the sign of peace."

This would be Sophie and Eli's signal to clamber onto the seat of the pew and "work the row," shaking hands with everyone behind them—"Peace be with you! Peace be with you!"—and getting in return all sorts of beneficent smiles and satisfying compliments on their in-church behavior. But they are not here, so instead Mike and I, our hands still linked, kiss each other on the lips, murmuring "Peace be with you," then turn to those around us. One thing I love about St. Patrick's is the ease with which people pass the peace. People grip one another's hands with both of theirs, hug each other, and even peck cheeks (Peggy again). I stoop and give Candy a hearty squeeze. I'm reminded of the warm-hearted monks who, despite their strict monastic regime, one-thousand-year-old clothing style, and ancient customs, are perfectly at ease embracing me and one another during this beautiful ritual.

As we pass the peace today, I realize something else that I haven't thought about before. Part of what we are doing here is helping take away one another's anxiety by giving each other a hand to hold, a shoulder to lean on, a reassuring kiss, all of which point toward and emulate Christ's healing presence among us. Peace I leave you, my peace I give you, he is telling us as we embrace.

Father Ken always extends this moment by walking up and down the aisles, enfolding people's hands in his warm and friendly paws. When he finally begins heading toward the front of the church, the little rustle of excitement that always makes its way through the congregation during peace passing begins to subside. We go quiet and turn expectantly toward the altar. For the rituals surrounding Communion—the moment we have all been waiting for—are about to begin.

Communing

The Co-Mingling; the Agnus Dei; Lord, I Am Not Worthy; Holy Communion

Yet even at this heightened moment, I am thinking of something else. And that is the way it often goes, for even as the Mass helps alleviate undue anxiety, it is constantly bumping up against my deepest loves and thus my deepest concerns.

Pretty much every Saturday morning since Mom died, my three sisters (Gail, Gretchen, and Tina) and I have faithfully Skyped at 7:30 a.m. PST. Our brother, Ron, totally refuses to join us, citing a natural-born horror of being stared at on a screen for a whole hour by four women in different parts of the USA. We punish him by making individual calls to him during the week just so he won't feel left out.

Tina, the youngest of us by a mile (in my case, as the oldest, by fourteen years) is the instigator of this new family tradition. It was Tina who Skyped with Mom nearly every day once she hit her eighties. It was Tina who flew back and forth from Cleveland to San Luis Obispo,

California, once Mom got sick. And it was Tina, classical pianist that she is, who bought an electronic keyboard to install in our mother's apartment, ostensibly to practice while she was in town but really in order to entertain Mom. In the very last hours of our mother's life, while all of us five siblings were gathered around the sickbed, it was Tina who went to the next room and played, one by one, Mom's favorites: Grieg, Schumann, Brahms, Chopin, Bach. Tina's logic regarding the Saturday morning Skype calls is that our mother was a sort of Grand Central Station for the five of us, the first-line responder in any sort of family crisis, keeping us informed as to our siblings' doings. Now that this is over, it is up to us to stay in touch.

She is right. Though we hate to admit it, even with the best of intentions it would be easy to drift apart. Life is full, after all, and we are busy people. Without that weekly face-to-face check-in, it would be nearly impossible for two Californians, one Minnesotan, and one Ohioan to stay in regular touch. But we have. Thank heaven. For just a week ago, in an emergency Skype call not on Saturday morning at 7:30 a.m. PST, we sisters got the news about Tina's cancer diagnosis.

Since that announcement, which has had us texting back and forth as she consults with specialists and looks at what the next phase might be for her, we have drawn even closer. For at this point in life, given that our gentle daddy died more than twenty years ago, we are what remain of the Original Nuclear Family. We live thousands of miles apart. Yet the five of us are still connected. In a certain way, we are even in communion. We worry about each other. We pass out unwanted free advice. We challenge one another (sometimes with a buzzing persistence) to be stronger, braver, healthier, calmer. Occasionally we have an online squabble and have to make up. We laugh together, mostly at ourselves. And according to Tina, all this is helping as at forty-eight she faces the possibility of an earlier death than any of us ever anticipated.

THE CO-MINGLING

As Kathy leads us into the Agnus Dei—"Lamb of God, you take away the sins of the world"—the Extraordinary Ministers come forward from their pews and gather in a semi-circle behind the altar. Father Ken begins breaking apart the large priest's host in what is called the fractioning rite, a ritual meant to call to mind the Last Supper when Jesus first broke the bread and handed it in pieces to his disciples. When he is finished, he drops a tiny piece of the consecrated bread into the chalice in the rite of "co-mingling." This small act, easy to miss, not only symbolizes the Resurrection but reminds us of those days in the early Church when a bit of the Eucharistic bread from the pope's own Mass (known as the *fermentum*) was distributed to the individual churches as a symbol of unity. It also harkens back to a time when small pieces of consecrated bread were soaked in the Precious Blood for those who, sick or dying, were unable to swallow well.[1]

THE AGNUS DEI

Meanwhile, one of the Extraordinary Ministers pours the Precious Blood into the chalices and another opens the golden tabernacle door and retrieves a *ciborium* (a plate-like vessel) of already-consecrated hosts in case they are needed, then distributes the newly blessed hosts into several ciboria. We are still singing the Agnus Dei:

> Lamb of God, you take away the sins of the world, have mercy on us.
> Lamb of God, you take away the sins of the world, have mercy on us.
> Lamb of God, you take away the sins of the world, grant us peace.

This brief and ancient hymn was originally meant to occupy what could be a long stretch while a whole loaf of bread was being fractioned. As the Church began to use pressed unleavened hosts instead, this process took much less time, and the Agnus Dei became more like a Communion hymn.[2]

As almost all hymns and prayers in the Mass do, the Agnus Dei comes straight from scripture. John the Baptist, at Jesus' request, baptizes him in the Jordan River. The next day when he sees Jesus walking toward him, John says to those standing nearby, "Behold, the Lamb of God, who takes away the sin of the world. He is the one of whom I said, 'A man is coming after me who ranks ahead of me because he existed before me.' I did not know him, but the reason why I came baptizing with water was that he might be made known to Israel." Then he adds, "I saw the Spirit come down like a dove from the sky and remain upon him. I did not know him, but the one who sent me to baptize with water told me, 'On whomever you see the Spirit come down and remain, he is the one who will baptize with the holy Spirit.' Now I have seen and testified that he is the Son of God" (Jn 1:29–33).

When we sing the Agnus Dei right before we partake of Communion, we are thus both looking back to the beginning of Jesus' public ministry, which is the baptism that takes place three years before his Crucifixion, and forward to the Pentecost, the descent of the Holy Spirit in individual tongues of fire upon the heads of the disciples fifty days after the Resurrection.

The Latin words of the Agnus Dei are particularly beautiful: *Agnus Dei, qui tollis peccata mundi: miserere nobis. Agnus Dei, qui tollis peccata mundi: dona nobis pacem.* I am always drawn to this last phrase—*dona nobis pacem* ("grant us peace")—even when I am singing the phrase in English because one of the ways my siblings and I formed the lifetime bond we are still guarding and keeping was as children doing dishes. Long before the advent of dishwashers, we stood before the kitchen sink on chairs and stools, our towels at the ready, while wet bowls and dishes and plates were passed our way. To make this onerous chore more palatable, Mom taught us to sing rounds; one of her favorites was called, simply, "Dona Nobis Pacem."

Fifty years later, during the long night of her dying, my sisters and I sang that round to her in the dark, then sang it again at her graveside service. And no matter how different we siblings are from one another—different in

personality, moral sensibility, aesthetic taste, political loyalty, religious belief; no matter how often we push too
hard or irritate one another with unasked for advice, all on
Skype, no less—this sung prayer from our distant childhood helps sustain our relationship. At this moment, as
the worrisome thought about Tina's cancer once again
rises within me, I consciously lean against the ancient
words: *dona nobis pacem*. Grant us peace.

Father Ken holds up the chalice and a piece of the
fractioned host, repeating the words of John the Baptist:

> Behold the Lamb of God,
> behold him who takes away the sins of the world.
> Blessed are those called to the supper of the Lamb.

LORD, I AM NOT WORTHY

We respond with more words from scripture:

> Lord, I am not worthy
> that you should enter under my roof,
> but only say the word
> and my soul shall be healed.

Over the centuries, different biblical allusions have
been used at this particular place in the Mass, but this
one, recently reinstated, was the first to be used by the
ancient Church:

> When [Jesus] entered Capernaum, a centurion
> approached him and appealed to him, saying,
> "Lord, my servant is lying at home paralyzed,
> suffering dreadfully." [Jesus] said to him, "I

will come and cure him." The centurion said in reply, "Lord, I am not worthy to have you enter under my roof; only say the word and my servant will be healed. For I too am a person subject to authority, with soldiers subject to me. And I say to one, 'Go,' and he goes; and to another, 'Come here,' and he comes; and to my slave, 'Do this,' and he does it." When Jesus heard this, he was amazed and said to those following him, "Amen, I say to you, in no one in Israel have I found such faith. I say to you, many will come from the east and the west, and will recline with Abraham, Isaac, and Jacob at the banquet in the kingdom of heaven, but the children of the kingdom will be driven out into outer darkness, where there will be wailing and grinding of teeth." And Jesus said to the centurion, "You may go; as you have believed, let it be done for you." And at that very hour [his] servant was healed.
(Mt 8:5–13)

HOLY COMMUNION

Now Father Ken consumes the host and drinks from his chalice before beginning the distribution of chalices and ciboria to those waiting in their semi-circle behind the altar. The words of the Communion song for the day appear on the overhead screen: "Shepherd me, O God, beyond my wants, beyond my fears, from death into life." Kathy leads us into the first verse ("God is my shepherd, there is nothing I shall want, I rest in the meadows of faithfulness and love") as the Extraordinary Ministers take their stations at the front of the sanctuary. The people in the first rows of each section begin to line up in front of either an EM or Father Ken.

Once again, here comes everybody. Or at least I wish that it were everybody. But some do not choose the Church, with its ancient rituals, its seemingly outdated worldview. Some, for their own reasons, cannot find it within themselves to believe. And this reality is reflected in the newer *Roman Missal* texts, which now say that the Precious Blood has been poured out "for many" rather than "for all." Which makes me sad but not because of any perceived harshness on the part of the Church. This is simply the truth, I have found, of life in the world. The Great Story does not move everyone in the way that it moves me.

But for those many who do respond to the call, Holy Communion makes all the difference. From the very first, to be a Christian has meant to be in communion with one's brothers and sisters in the Eucharistic meal. Communion comes from the Greek word *koinonia*, which in ancient times generally referred to familial ties. From the moment of Jesus' Death and Resurrection, this is what we now were: a newborn spiritual family, united by our mutual partaking of the Body and Blood of Christ. The Gospel of Luke, for example, tells the story of two disciples who meet a man on the road to Emmaus just hours after they have been to the empty tomb and seen for themselves that the body truly is missing. He asks them what they are talking about. They can't believe he doesn't know.

Hasn't everybody in Jerusalem heard about the Crucifixion of their revered prophet and teacher? And now, it seems, he has risen from the dead, though that is almost impossible to imagine. The stranger proceeds to interpret scripture for them—all the many prophecies in the Old Testament, beginning with Moses, who pointed toward just this moment.

They listen, enrapt, and when they get to their destination and the mysterious man looks as if he is continuing on, they invite him to stay with them instead. "And it happened that, while he was with them at table, he took bread, said the blessing, broke it and gave it to them. With that their eyes were opened and they recognized him, but he vanished from their sight. Then they said to each other, 'Were not our hearts burning [within us] while he spoke to us on the way and opened the scriptures to us?'" (Lk 24:30–32). Filled with joy, they rush back to Jerusalem to tell the other disciples that they have met and conversed with the Risen Lord. "Then the two recounted what had taken place on the way and *how he was made known to them in the breaking of the bread*" (Lk 24:35, italics mine).[3]

Two thousand years later, we Catholics are still participating in the same divine meal instituted by Jesus on the night he was betrayed. According to the *Catechism*, the fruits of Communion are many: "The principal fruit of receiving the Eucharist in Holy Communion is an intimate union with Christ Jesus" (*CCC*, 1391). More, we are receiving real food: "What material food produces in our bodily life, Holy Communion wonderfully achieves in our spiritual life" (*CCC*, 1392). In addition, "*Holy Communion separates us from sin*," cleansing us from past venial sins, strengthening the bonds of love within us, and making it much harder to fall into mortal sin later (*CCC*, 1393). The Eucharist also binds Catholics together in the "*Mystical Body of Christ*"; in so doing, it literally "*makes the Church*" (*CCC*, 1396). More, "*the Eucharist commits us to the poor*," the very least of our brothers, for it is in the poor that we recognize the face of Christ with whom we are communing (*CCC*, 1397). And finally, our participation in the Eucharist reminds us of the divisions among ourselves and non-Catholic Christians, with whom we cannot yet share the table, and urges us to keep praying for total healing and reconciliation (*CCC*, 1398).[4]

But beyond what the Eucharist provides for us in terms of spiritual food or fortification against sin, it also initiates something we rarely think about otherwise: sacred time. As Romano Guardini puts it, "To participate properly in the Mass it is essential that we be aware of its temporalness: of its beginning, continuation, and end. [Yet] this brief portion of time enfolds eternity."[5] Thus, Holy Communion is also where we experience kairos.

As I enter the slow line moving forward toward the altar, I think back to that first Mass I ever attended, and how it was this moment—Communion—that struck me more than any other: the bows that some of the people made before the Body and Blood of Christ, the crossing of chests and murmured "Amens," the look of inwardness and private joy on the faces of those returning to their pews. I am sure that it was this that finally made me Catholic: the witnessing of the Lord's Supper as it was meant to be celebrated; the charge in the air; the sense of a great love radiating from the front of the church and gathering strength as it billowed out the doors to the world beyond. I have spoken to many other converts over the years, including Kathy the cantor, who all say the same thing: It was the Eucharist that did it. The Real Presence of Christ. The only moment, on this side of the veil, in which Jesus is physically accessible to us. Tasting for ourselves the sweetness of a deep, abiding, and transcendental unity.[6]

I can sense my husband close behind me as we approach the altar; never will this hard-won spiritual intimacy of ours stop seeming like a miracle. I glance beside me and see a woman who has attended Mass for decades without becoming Catholic; not able to partake, she is crossing her arms as a silent signal that she would still love to be blessed. And here is ninety-two-year-old Bert, who refuses to be served in the row set aside for the sick and the disabled, jamming his walker into the carpet as he comes, while behind him files an entire extended ranching family. There is the man with the small gray ponytail. There is the woman who always wears jeans. There is the girl whose husband is in prison. There is the father whose only son is paralyzed for life. Trailing clouds of glory do we come, from God who is our home, as Wordsworth put it.

And now I am standing before Eli's longtime teacher Joycie, who loves all her grandchildren so very much but especially the one who needs it the most, and I am making a bow, and she is holding up the host and saying to me in her soft voice, "The Body of Christ," and I am cupping my hands like a small throne, and she is placing it there for me to eat, and I am saying "Amen" and laying the host on my tongue, where it is dissolving just as my life on this earth is dissolving. Just like all our lives, including the lives of those I love so much it hurts. Returning not to the worms and the soil in the ancient pagan way or according to the contemporary doctrine of scientism but instead to the homeland of our hope.

Then I take a few steps to the left, where Joycie's husband Mikey is waiting for me, the two of them not only marriage partners but teaching partners for thirty-five years, and I am holding out my hand for the chalice, which he is handing to me while murmuring, "The Blood of Christ," and I am tipping it against my lips and sipping the Precious Blood and handing it back to him, and he is wiping the edge with the purificator and smiling at me, and I am crossing myself once again, whispering "Amen." And then I am walking dazedly back to our pew.

Sometimes when I get there I kneel for a few minutes. Father Bernard, the wry little French-Canadian monk who dragged Jesus out the door with him whenever he left his cell, taught me that the Eucharistic meal should be savored for as long as possible, that the moments after receiving are especially filled with grace. Today, instead, I stand in the ancient posture of adoration, facing Christ on the altar. Please, I say to him. Please heal my sister Tina as you healed so many in Galilee. Please bring her back to full and complete health. Please strengthen and sustain her as she goes through this upcoming surgery. Please keep her from being too frightened. And please give me the wisdom not to say dumb things to her when we Skype next Saturday morning at 7:30 a.m. PST. I ask all this in your Most Holy Name.

Amen. *Dona nobis pacem*. Grant us peace.

Going Forth

The Prayer after Communion, the Final Blessing and Sending Forth, the Recessional

The last person has communed, and the Extraordinary Ministers have, one by one, returned to the altar. Whatever is left in the chalices, they discretely drink. Then they carefully wipe out each vessel with a purificator before returning it to the tray. Leftover hosts are carefully brushed into one of the ciboria and placed back inside the Tabernacle. The empty vessels are returned to the credence table. The last trace of the sacred meal has been removed.

PRAYER AFTER COMMUNION

Father Ken returns to his chair and, hands on the armrests, bows his head and closes his eyes. Those who have been kneeling or standing now sit. Silence fills the sanctuary. This is the time of thanksgiving for what we have received. One of the traditional prayers employed by

Catholics during this grace-filled moment is the *Anima Christi*:

> Soul of Christ, sanctify me.
> Body of Christ, save me.
> Blood of Christ, inebriate me.
> Water from Christ's side, wash me.
> Passion of Christ, strengthen me.
> O good Jesus, hear me.
> Within thy wounds, hide me.
> Suffer me not to be separated from Thee.
> From the malicious enemy, defend me.
> In the hour of my death, call me
> And bid me come unto Thee
> That I may praise Thee with Thy saints
> And with Thy angels
> forever and ever.
> Amen.

As Jungmann puts it, "What we have received is called a holy gift, a heavenly banquet, spiritual nourishment, an efficacious mystery, the Holy Body and the Precious Blood."[1] And we are thankful. But we are also human, and we know how quickly the effects of this great sacramental mystery can dissipate in our little cubicles under the fluorescent office lights or just like that when we are dragging the overflowing trash cans to the curbside or as we dutifully measure out our daily dose of insulin. Daily life can flatten us. We can forget. Too much loss can tempt us toward despair. And therefore this moment of thanksgiving quickly merges into something else: petition. "What we expect and implore from our partaking of the

Body and Blood of Christ is the progress and final triumph of its efficacy in us," in Jungmann's words.[2] We want this to work. We implore that it will.

Father Ken stands. Peter brings him the *Sacramentary*, the liturgical book of prayers used by the priest, holding it up so he can read the final prayer. He prays.

We answer with an "Amen."

Then he clears his throat and says, "There are a few announcements." He reads from his notes, hidden in a beautiful leather binder. There will be a blood drive next Sunday. The Altar Guild is looking for volunteers. The youth will be making a retreat. Calorie-free donuts will be served in the parish hall after the Mass.

FINAL BLESSING AND SENDING FORTH

When all has been announced, he closes his notebook and says, "The Lord be with you."

We respond, "And with your spirit."

He raises his right hand over us and we bow from the waist. "May almighty God bless you, the Father, and the Son (here, he makes the Sign of the Cross) and the Holy Spirit."

Again we say, "Amen."

Then he says, "Go forth, the Mass is ended."

And we say, "Thanks be to God."

We are officially done. All has been accomplished. It is time for us to return to the world. May God protect and sustain us as we do.

THE BREAKFAST CLUB

As usual, I am mentally halfway out the door, my hungry belly having made its presence known as soon as Father Ken mentioned those calorie-free donuts. Catholics are supposed to fast before they partake, and since I have been up since five thirty, I'm feeling the lack of breakfast. In fact, I am already running through the menu at Francisco's Country Kitchen in my head; this morning, I am leaning toward a side of refried beans and corn tortillas. And of course, looking forward to time with our friends.

The after-Mass breakfast club—Joe, Cindy, Bill, Lynnette, Mike, me, and Mary, who despite her most Catholic of names, for deeply personal reasons has found it impossible to attend Mass for many years now—came into being not as a Christian fellowship enterprise, a Bible study, or a religious discussion group but as something else altogether.

At times, it is true, one of us (usually Bill) will bring up a point from Father Ken's homily and we will bat that around for a while, Mary asking for clarification when needed. Usually we discuss movies or upcoming travels or the rare local political scandal instead. A few years back, when everybody's elderly parents seemed to be dying at the same time, we talked about assisted living and gerontological toenail care and hospice and cremation versus burial. If ever we are joined by some of our grandchildren, as when breakfast club emeriti Eli and Sophie make a guest appearance, we are quite easily steered into the realm of soccer, Star Wars Lego sets, and the wonderful world of kittens.

Yet year after year, we remain mysteriously connected. Though I have never raised the topic over our Light Bites and beans so have no idea what my fellow breakfast-clubbers think—or even whether they feel it, too—I believe it is our shared Catholicism, the peculiar religious milieu in which we live and move and experience ourselves as spiritual beings, that holds us together.

As contemporary Catholics, we live in the same world that everybody else does. We are fully aware of the hot-button issues of our era. Yet for the most part (and with the exception of our friend Mary), we have no major beefs with the Church. We are not, for example, irate about the likely fact that we will never see women priests in our time, even though Lynnette, at least, would really like to see that happen. Neither do we spend much time talking about abortion and gay marriage and physician-assisted suicide. I am just guessing about my fellow clubbers here—maybe they would differ—but I think we correctly perceive that these issues are not primarily political but personal: that they arise within sad, complex, vulnerable situations that require from us wisdom, compassion, and love rather than fiery polemics.

In regard to the Church scandals of the past few decades, like all Catholics, we were appalled. At the same time we are not convinced that it was ever the massive, systemic problem it is too often portrayed to be. Why not? Because we ourselves have respected and loved so many wonderful priests who have never broken their vows, who for the love of God have given up their lives in order to serve us. And when we are told that the Church is a corrupt medieval artifact that needs to go away once and for all, we don't buy it because we have been privileged to know Sister Regina and Sister Eva and the other Sisters of Mercy who came to Arroyo Grande from Ireland in their early twenties and devoted the next forty-plus years to our spiritual care.

Our view of Catholicism, in other words, comes from the ground up. Week after week, year after year, we practice the religion we believe in. Though every one of us in the breakfast club has faced troubling questions along the way, including serious doubts, we continue to show up at Mass. We come because, as Joe puts it, "When I take Communion, I have Christ in me."

You'd never pick this up from the casual camaraderie at our table, but it's hard to let each other go on Sunday mornings after Mass. Though I'm not sure exactly why, I suspect this has to do with a heightened, post-Eucharistic sense of our existential fragility. We have just spent those moments in kairos time. We have just partaken of Holy Communion, surrounded by that cloud of witnesses— generations of Christians who were born, like us, into the same beautiful world, who lived and loved and wept and died. And each Sunday brings closer our own inevitable parting from one another. It is the Mass, not our busy daily lives, that reveals this reality with such startling clarity. Earthly life, even in *Sunset* magazine's version of paradise, is not forever.

And so we hug goodbye in the parking lot as though sending each other off to an alien land.

THE RECESSIONAL

Kathy steps to the podium, dragging me back from my breakfast reverie. The piano starts to play. The overhead screen displays the words, "Let there be peace on earth, and let it begin with me." As we sing, "Let there be peace on earth, the peace that was meant to be," Lectors Larry and Pat come to the front of the church. Raphael, Father Ken, and his faithful helper Peter, carrying the crucifix, all face the altar. At the beginning of the second verse—"Let peace begin with me, let this be the moment now"—they bow in unison, then turn toward the congregation.

Today, and only for this moment because I know I will forget again, I can see what's been bugging me these past few months. I get what's been causing that existential broodiness of mine, that persistent gray mood that followed me to Mass today. It's death, pure and simple. I'm tired of it. I don't want to go through more of it. But it's not going to stop happening, for this is what it means to love and be mortal. And thus my only hope is hope, which makes me think of one of my favorite passages from Isaiah:

> Then the wolf shall be a guest of the lamb,
> and the leopard shall lie down with the young goat;
> The calf and the young lion shall browse together,
> with a little child to guide them.
> The cow and the bear shall graze,
> together their young shall lie down;
> the lion shall eat hay like the ox.
> The baby shall play by the viper's den,
> and the child lay his hand on the adder's lair.

They shall not harm or destroy on all my holy
     mountain;
for the earth shall be filled with knowledge of the
     LORD,
as water covers the sea.
(Is 11:6–9)

That's what I want—no more death or dying, no more
suffering or despair, my tears to be turned to dancing—
but for that I will have to wait. We are on the way, but we
are not there yet.

The recessional begins. We are still singing: "With God
as our Father, brothers all are we; Let me walk with my
brother, in perfect harmony." Singing, we cross ourselves
as the cross goes by us.

This is what we have. This is what we know. This is
what we love. Go in peace to love and serve the Lord.
Thanks be to God.

Epilogue

Exactly one year has passed since I sat in the pew at St. Patrick's, taking notes for this book. Last night there were fireworks (the Fourth of July) and this morning we are once again celebrating the Fourteenth Sunday in Ordinary Time. For this is how the ancient cycle of Church life unfolds: over and over, we return to the places we have been. Year after year, we relive the events of the Great Story, the Story of the Human Race, honoring what should be honored, weeping for what should be mourned, and praising God for his infinite love.

I remember what was on my mind this time last year— the news that my sister Tina had cancer. Shortly after that, she underwent surgery and many weeks of radiation. We sisters recently got the news during our Saturday morning Skype call that her follow-up mammogram was clear and that she is feeling good, if still somewhat tired from the treatments. That she is looking forward to seeing everybody soon when we rendezvous in the Cascades for our annual sibling backpack. That it looks as though she will make it to fifty after all.

Almost everybody who was on duty during that Mass a year ago is back: young Peter as altar-server; Mikey and

Joycie as EMs; and Pat, who on this day last year was a Lector, as an EM too, despite the fact that she is once again in chemotherapy after what seemed like a miraculous healing. Every time she goes in for another round of the drugs, she sends an e-mail to her large circle of friends. I believe that these e-mails of hers are in some way akin to the Epistles of the New Testament. Like the letters of Saint Paul, they are always surprising, invariably challenging, and reliably reassuring. They are teaching us how to handle adversity with courage and faith.

The only person missing during this one-year-later Mass is Father Ken.

The last time I saw him as himself—all six feet two of him, in all his booming good health—was the Sunday after Easter. I was Lector #1 that day, which meant I was carrying the beautiful Book of the Gospels in the opening processional. As we lined up in the foyer of the church, waiting for Father Ken to give Kathy the signal to begin, I squeezed Peter's shoulder and he grinned back at me, hoisting the heavy processional cross a little higher. People were still streaming past us, and both I and the other Lector kept smiling and grasping their hands as they went by: "Good morning! Good morning!"

Suddenly, I realized that Father Ken, robed in the white of Eastertide—the color that most set off his handsome African American skin and eyes, which I pointed out pretty much every time he wore white and gold vestments—was beckoning to me, and I went to the back of the processional line to see what he wanted. "I keep forgetting to tell you. You need to speak up a little louder," he said. "Your voice is soft. The old people can't hear you. Don't be afraid of the mic."

"No?" I said. "I was told not to touch it or it would go crazy. That feedback thing."

"You can touch it," he said. "Pull it closer to your mouth."

"Okay," I said. "And by the way, how are you doing after the whole Easter Triduum?" Easter in the Catholic Church is traditionally a killer for priests. Service after service, and one of them—Easter Vigil—lasting late into the night. In years past, he'd fully admitted to being exhausted by the end of it.

He laughed, that big, easy, New Orleans laugh that came from deep in the center of his belly. "Easter was fine," he said. "Amazingly fine. I must be getting better at this. But still and all, I'm ready for a good long nap."

"Well, I hope you get one this week," I said. "You need it."

Two days later, he was transported to the emergency room at Arroyo Grande Hospital at four in the morning. A few hours later he underwent open heart surgery in San Luis Obispo for a ruptured aortic aneurysm. I got the call that evening. The good news was that he had survived a catastrophic physical event that kills 75 to 90 percent of those it strikes. The bad news was that he was not coming out of the anesthesia. And he continued to sleep for the next three days.

When he finally awoke in the intensive care unit, he could not breathe on his own for more than a few hours before beginning to struggle for air, so he had to stay on the ventilator. During the coming days, his condition did not improve. And it began to be clear that his brain had suffered a major injury caused by severe oxygen deprivation during the rupture of the aneurysm.

Five and a half weeks later, he died in ICU, having turned sixty-six while he lay in bed still unable to speak or breathe on his own. His sisters Denise and Julie were at his bedside. Denise, a long-time ICU nurse herself, took a medical leave from her job in New Orleans in order to accompany her brother through this extended time of waiting. Mike and I were privileged to spend an hour with him several days before he passed away. Though he was in a deep sleep at this point, we were able to pray with him, to tell him that we loved him, to thank him for being such a good friend and priest, and to assure him that eye has not seen and ear has not heard the wonders that awaited him next.

That was a comforting moment for both of us. Yet these kinds of reassurances can trip too easily off our tongues if we're not careful. In times of great sorrow, it's tempting to fall back on platitudes, to parrot what we've heard in church, to resist the reality of what's happening in front of us. For despite the sentimental accounts of beautiful, saintly deaths, witnessing this great transition firsthand can be a harrowing experience. And realizing that a permanent hole has opened up in our own lives—that this wound of grief will be with us forever—can feel almost unbearable, at least initially.

For some weeks after Father Ken's hospitalization and death, I had to force myself to go to 7:30 a.m. Mass at St.

Patrick's. It was simply too painful. I kept waiting for him to come singing up the aisle or to pick up the Book of the Gospels and hold it on high or to step up to the ambo to deliver one of his Louisiana-flavored homilies. But he wasn't coming back, and that has taken a long time to accept—not only for me but for Mike and hundreds of other parishioners at St. Patrick's. As someone who first received the call to the priesthood in his early twenties but only followed up on it thirty-some years later, Father Ken radiated the joy of a man who had finally found his true vocation. And that joy was infectious. It's what we most miss about him.

Since his passing, I have noticed how often the word *death* comes up during my daily psalm reading, as though an awareness of mortality must undergird every moment of our existence. Hard as it has been to accept while still in a state of mourning, I am slowly coming back to what I've always known: that the acknowledgment of our finitude is part of the deep wisdom of the Bible, not to mention a defining feature of Christianity. Our mortality is part of what it means to be human. Of the varied creatures who abide on this earth, we are the only ones aware that death awaits us all. And when we try to avoid this painful fact, we can become obsessed with survival at any cost, and our lives can become subtly distorted. We can lose the boldness of our faith, our willingness to love deeply, to take joy in the present moment, to hope. Gil Bailie says that when we become entranced by death, we lose out on the precious gift of our "holy actuality"—which means the blessing of living as the person we really are, instead of in idolatrous fantasy.[1]

The mystic Adrienne von Speyr adds that it is only the experience of our own finitude that allows us to grasp God's infinity; it is only our recognition that earthly life will end, no doubt before we are ready, that allows us to envision eternal life. And thus, hard as it is to fathom, death is in the long run a difficult but liberating blessing.[2] Knowing that our lives have this built-in endpoint to them—that we, too, will soon be passing from this world on our way to another kind of existence—imbues our daily round with profound meaning. Time's a'wasting. There is work to be done. There are people to love. There are prayers to be said, and there is the great mystery of the Mass to celebrate.

So here I am, once again sitting in the pew on the Fourteenth Sunday in Ordinary Time. Kathy has already led us in the opening song as Peter and the crucifix and the two Lectors and our interim pastor processed up the aisle. The Book of Gospels has been placed on the altar. And now Father Jim, a warm and witty Irishman who served St. Patrick's twenty years ago and at seventy has rushed back to be with us during this suspended moment between the death of our beloved pastor and the installation of whomever will be sent to us next, is standing before us.

"In the name of the Father and the Son and the Holy Spirit," he says as we cross ourselves in the ancient way. I look at him up there, a priest who thought he was done with us, but who instead has come back to love us and guide us through this time of mourning. Who gives us hope, as we who are part of the Mystical Body of Christ give each other hope, that the ongoing life of the Church does not depend on any single person, no matter how precious. That Father Ken—that any one of us—can go safely through the great transition, knowing the rest of us will be okay.

"Grace to you and peace from God our Father and the Lord Jesus Christ," says Father Jim with his Irish lilt on this foggy morning in *Sunset* magazine's version of paradise. I think of Father Ken's favorite poem, "God's Grandeur," and the Holy Spirit who broods over this world with, ah, bright wings.

Yes, I think. When it comes down to it, this is why we are here. For grace and for peace. And thanks be to God who bestows them upon us like manna, each day there for the finding.

Acknowledgments

No book is ever the result of an entirely individual effort, but *One Ordinary Sunday* was truly a collaborative project. My undying gratitude goes to Ave Maria Press's publisher, Tom Grady, who first conceived the notion of a lay-written book about a real Mass on a real Sunday in a real parish and asked me if I'd be interested in writing it. He then spent over a year helping me revise and re-revise the ten introductory pages that would best encapsulate what we were trying to accomplish. It was Tom who shipped me Joseph A. Jungmann's massive two-volume history of the Mass, Tom who introduced me to the work of Mike Aquilina on the early Christian Church, and Tom who suggested other key scholars along the way. When I finally sent in the first draft of the manuscript, it was Tom who took on the editing role despite a detached retina that kept him from reading anything for nearly three months. Without Tom's major investment of intellectual and creative energy in this project, I doubt I would have had the self-confidence to take it on at all.

I also owe a great debt of thanks to the many others who helped me write this book. To breakfast club members Bill and Lynnette Borgman, Joe and Cindy

Giambalvo, and Mary Giambalvo, all of whom graciously allowed themselves to be grilled on any number of Catholic-related topics while trying to eat in peace, my deepest gratitude for your forbearance. To Ken Walker, who read and critiqued the chapters that gave me the most trouble, thank you for that and for the many other ways you have helped me think better over the years. To Fr. Isaiah Tiechert, my longtime confessor and spiritual director, my deepest appreciation for your counsel during my struggles to get through this project and for sending me key books along the way. To friends and readers Susie Miner and Karen Lake-Shampain, my most sincere gratitude for your many good suggestions. To Msgr. Michael Heintz; Fr. Jim Nisbet; Fr. Thomas Matus, O.S.B. Cam.; and Fr. Thomas Jones, C.S.C.; who carefully checked the manuscript for potentially confusing or misleading statements, thank you for investing so much of your time and energy in a project not your own. To my fellow parishioners at St. Patrick's Church in Arroyo Grande, thank you for allowing me to write about you in ways you never planned. To Denise Lacey and Julie Brown, whose deep faith helped me cope with the entirely unexpected death of my dear friend and pastor Fr. Ken Brown, you will always be my sisters in Christ.

And finally, to my long-suffering husband and best friend, Mike, whose steady encouragement means everything to me, may God bless you for your staunch and loyal love.

Notes

PREFACE

1. Paul VI, *Mysterium Fidei*; AAS, 57, 1965, 762 (no. 32), quoted in James T. O'Connor, *The Hidden Manna: A Theology of the Eucharist* (San Francisco: Ignatius, 1988), 262.

PART I

INTRODUCTION

1. Kenneth Barker, ed., *NIV Study Bible* (Grand Rapids, MI: Zondervan, 1985), 781.

GATHERING

1. Joseph A. Jungmann, S.J., *The Mass of the Roman Rite: Its Origins and Development,* trans. Francis A. Brunner (Notre Dame, IN: Christian Classics, 2012), 1:159.

2. The quoted words are paraphrased from Antonio Rosmini, *Of the Five Wounds of the Holy Church,* trans. Henry Parry Liddon (London: Rivingtons, 1883), 24–25.

3. Jungmann, *Mass of the Roman Rite,* 1:161.

4. John Paul II, *Ordinatio Sacerdotalis,* 1994.

5. Romano Guardini, *The Spirit of the Liturgy,* trans. Ada Lane (New York: Crossroad, 1998), 71.

6. Joseph Cardinal Ratzinger, quoted in Guardini, *Spirit of the Liturgy*, 14.

PREPARING

1. Jungmann, *Mass of the Roman Rite*, 1:346.

2. Michael Dubruiel, *The How-To Book of the Mass: Everything You Need to Know But No One Ever Taught You* (Huntington, IN: Our Sunday Visitor, 2006), 82; see also Jungmann, *Mass of the Roman Rite*, 1:376.

REMEMBERING

1. See Elizabeth Scalia, *Strange Gods: Unmasking the Idols in Everyday Life* (Notre Dame: Ave Maria Press, 2013) for a fuller discussion of this subject.

2. Jungmann, *Mass of the Roman Rite*, 1:398.

3. Ibid., 1:392–393.

4. Dubruiel, *How-To Book of the Mass*, 94–96.

RESPONDING

1. Dom Paul Delatte, Abbott of Solesmes and Superior-General of the Congregation of Benedictines in France, *Commentary on the Rule of St. Benedict*, trans. Dom Justin McCann (Latrobe, PA: The Archabbey Press, 2000), 183

2. Dubruiel, *How-To Book of the Mass*, 106.

3. Jungmann, *Mass of the Roman Rite*, 1:422–423.

4. Ibid., 1:426.

5. Barker, *NIV Study Bible*, 782.

6. Peter-Damian Belisle, O.S.B. Cam., *The Privilege of Love: Camaldolese Benedictine Spirituality* (Collegeville, MN: Liturgical, 2002), 87.

7. John Paul II, *The Encyclicals in Everyday Language*, ed. Joseph G. Donders (Maryknoll, NY: Orbis, 2005), 40.

8. Francis, *Misericordiae Vultus*, section 12, April 11, 2015, https://w2.vatican.va/content/francesco/en/apost_letters/documents/papa-francesco_bolla_20150411_misericordiae-vultus.html

RECONNECTING

1. Dubruiel, *How-To Book of the Mass*, 112.

RESURRECTING

1. Sofia Cavalletti, *The Religious Potential of the Child: Experiencing Scripture and Liturgy with Young Children*, trans. Patricia M. Coulter and Julie M. Coulter (Chicago: Catechesis of the Good Shepherd Publications, 1998), 44.

2. Ibid., 44.
3. Ibid., 15.
4. Jungmann, *Mass of the Roman Rite*, 1:435.
5. Ibid., 1:454.
6. Ibid., 1:448–449.

LISTENING

1. *Preaching the Mystery of Faith: The Sunday Homily* (Washington, DC: United States Conference of Catholic Bishops, 2012), 30.

2. Jungmann, *Mass of the Roman Rite*, 1:458.
3. Ibid., 1:459.
4. Gerard Manley Hopkins, "God's Grandeur," in *Gerard Manley Hopkins: A Critical Edition of the Major Works*, ed. Catherine Phillips (Oxford: Oxford University Press, 1986), 128.

DECLARING

1. Luke Timothy Johnson, *The Creed: What Christians Believe and Why It Matters* (New York: Doubleday, 2003), 33.

2. C. S. Lewis, introduction to *On the Incarnation*, by Athanasius, trans. and ed. Religious of the Community of St. Mary the Virgin (Crestwood, NY: St. Vladimir's Seminary Press, 2012), 9.

3. Johnson, *The Creed*, 231.

INTERCEDING

1. John Paul II, *Encyclicals in Everyday Language*, 243.

2. Gil Bailie, "The Subject of *Guadium Et Spes*: Reclaiming a Christocentric Anthropology of the Human Person" (Sonoma, CA: The Cornerstone Forum, 2005), 23, https://www.stthomas.edu/media/catholicstudies/center/johnaryaninstitute/conferences/2005-vatican/Bailie.pdf.

3. Jungmann, *Mass of the Roman Rite*, 1:480.

4. Dubruiel, *How-To Book of the Mass*, 150–151.

PART II

INTRODUCTION

1. William Wordsworth, "Ode," in *William Wordsworth*, ed. Stephen Gill (Oxford: Oxford University Press, 1984), 297.

2. Hopkins, *Gerard Manley Hopkins*, 128.

3. Mike Aquilina, *The Mass of the Early Christians*, 2nd ed. (Huntington, IN: Our Sunday Visitor, 2007), 43.

OFFERING

1. Jungmann, *Mass of the Roman Rite*, 2:1–2.

2. Ibid., 2:10.

3. Ibid., 2:6.

4. Ibid., 2:11.

5. Ibid., note on 2:23.

6. Ibid., 2:15.

7. Ibid., 2:27.

8. Ibid., 2:37.

9. Dubruiel, *How-To Book of the Mass*, 160.

10. Ibid.

11. Jungmann, *Mass of the Roman Rite*, 2:76.

12. Ibid., 2:77.

13. Dubruiel, *How-To Book of the Mass*, 162–163.

14. Rudolf Otto, *The Idea of the Holy*, trans. John W. Harvey (London: Oxford University Press, 1971), 12.

PRAISING

1. Jungmann, *Mass of the Roman Rite*, 1:363.

2. Quoted in Dubruiel, *How-To Book of the Mass*, 169.

3. Mike Aquilina, *Mass of the Early Christians*, 35.

4. Ibid., 20, 220.

5. Ibid., 63–64.

6. Ibid., 66.

7. Ibid., 68.

8. Ibid., 33.

9. Quoted in Jungmann, *Mass of the Roman Rite*, 2:22.

10. Quoted in Aquilina, *Mass of the Early Christians*, 33.

11. Jungmann, *Mass of the Roman Rite*, 2:32.

12. Ibid., 2:115.

13. See Jungmann, *Mass of the Roman Rite*, 2:132; also Joseph Cardinal Ratzinger, *The Spirit of the Liturgy* (San Francisco: Ignatius Press, 2014), 66.

14. Quoted in Ratzinger, *Spirit of the Liturgy*, 66.

KNEELING

1. Aquilina, *Mass of the Early Christians*, 65.

2. Jungmann, *Mass of the Roman Rite*, 2:150.

ASSENTING

1. Joseph Cardinal Ratzinger, *God Is Near Us: The Eucharist, the Heart of Life*, trans. Henry Taylor, eds. Steven Otto Horn and Vinzenz Pfnur (San Francisco: Ignatius, 2001), 84–85.

2. Ibid.

3. Flannery O'Connor, *The Habit of Being: Letters of Flannery O'Connor*, ed. Sally Fitzgerald (New York: Farrar, Straus and Giroux, 1979), 125.

4. Quoted in John Paul II, *Encyclicals in Everyday Language*, 362.

5. C. S. Lewis, *Miracles: A Preliminary Study* (San Francisco: HarperOne, 2001), 221.

6. Sofia Cavalletti, *Living Liturgy: Elementary Reflections*, trans. Patricia M. Coulter and Julie M. Coulter (Chicago: Catechesis of the Good Shepherd Publications, 1998), 95.

PRAYING

1. Cavalletti, *Living Liturgy*, 101.

2. Tertullian, quoted in *Catechism of the Catholic Church*, 2761.

3. Jungmann, *Mass of the Roman Rite*, 2:323.

4. Quoted in Dubruiel, *How-To Book of the Mass*, 194.

5. Jungmann, *Mass of the Roman Rite*, 2:328–329.

COMMUNING

1. Dubruiel, *How-To Book of the Mass*, 200.

2. Ibid., 198.

3. Scott Hahn, *The Lamb's Supper: The Mass as Heaven on Earth* (New York: Doubleday, 1999), 29.

4. Dubruiel, *How-To Book of the Mass*, 209.

5. Romano Guardini, *Meditations before Mass* (Notre Dame, IN: Christian Classics, 2014), 60.

6. O'Connor, *The Hidden Manna*, 287.

GOING FORTH

1. Jungmann, *Mass of the Roman Rite*, 2:423.

2. Ibid., 2:423.

EPILOGUE

1. Gil Bailie, "Gil Bailie's Reflections on the Divine Comedy, Dante's *Inferno* Part 5" (lecture), downloadable MP3 audio file (Sonoma, CA: The Cornerstone Forum, 1995).

2. Adrienne von Speyr, *The Boundless God*, trans. Helen M. Tomko (San Francisco: Ignatius, 2004), 23.

Bibliography

Titles marked with an asterisk (*) were especially valuable in the writing of this book.

*Aquilina, Mike. *The Mass of the Early Christians.* 2nd ed. Huntington, IN: Our Sunday Visitor, 2007.

Athanasius, St. *On the Incarnation.* Translated and edited by a Religious of the Community of St. Mary the Virgin. Introduction by C. S. Lewis. Crestwood, NY: St. Vladimir's Seminary Press, 2012.

Bailie, Gil. *Violence Unveiled: Humanity at the Crossroads.* New York: Crossroad, 1999.

Belisle, Peter-Damian, O.S.B. Cam. *The Privilege of Love: Camaldolese Benedictine Spirituality.* Collegeville, MN: Liturgical, 2002.

Boersma, Hans. *Heavenly Participation: The Weaving of a Sacramental Tapestry.* Grand Rapids, MI: Eerdmans, 2011.

Borella, Jean. *The Sense of the Supernatural.* Translated by G. John Champoux. Edinburgh: T&T Clark, 1998.

Catechism of the Catholic Church. 2nd edition. Washington, DC: United States Catholic Conference, 1997.

Cavalletti, Sofia. *Living Liturgy: Elementary Reflections*. Translated by Patricia M. Coulter and Julie M. Coulter. Chicago: Catechesis of the Good Shepherd Publications, 1998.

————. *The Religious Potential of the Child: Experiencing Scripture and Liturgy with Young Children*. Translated by Patricia M. Coulter and Julie M. Coulter. Chicago: Liturgy Training Publications, 1992.

Copleston, F. C. *Aquinas: An Introduction to the Life and Work of the Great Medieval Thinker*. New York: Penguin, 1956.

*Dubruiel, Michael. *The How-To Book of the Mass: Everything You Need to Know But No One Ever Taught You*. Huntington, IN: Our Sunday Visitor, 2006.

Eberstadt, Mary. *Adam and Eve after the Pill: Paradoxes of the Sexual Revolution*. San Francisco: Ignatius, 2012.

Flynn, Gabriel, and Paul D. Murray, eds. *Ressourcement: A Movement for Renewal in Twentieth-Century Catholic Theology*. New York: Oxford University Press, 2014.

Gilson, Etienne. *Thomist Realism and the Critique of Knowledge*. Translated by Mark A. Wauck. San Francisco: Ignatius, 1986.

*Guardini, Romano. *Meditations before Mass*. Translated by Eleanor Castendyk Briefs. Notre Dame, IN: Ave Maria Press, 2014.

*————. *The Spirit of the Liturgy*. Translated by Ada Lane. New York: Crossroad, 1998.

*Hahn, Scott. *The Lamb's Supper: The Mass as Heaven on Earth*. New York: Doubleday, 1999.

Hahn, Scott, and Kimberly Hahn. *Rome Sweet Home: Our Journey to Catholicism*. San Francisco: Ignatius, 1993.

Hopkins, Gerard Manley. *Gerard Manley Hopkins: A Critical Edition of the Major Works*. Edited by Catherine Phillips. Oxford: Oxford University Press, 1986.

Howard, Thomas. *Evangelical Is Not Enough*. Nashville: Thomas Nelson, 1984.

———. *On Being Catholic*. San Francisco: Ignatius, 1997.

Jenkins, Philip. *The New Anti-Catholicism: The Last Acceptable Prejudice*. New York: Oxford University Press, 2003.

John Paul II. *The Encyclicals in Everyday Language*. Edited by Joseph G. Donders. Maryknoll, NY: Orbis, 2005.

*Johnson, Luke Timothy. *The Creed: What Christians Believe and Why It Matters*. New York: Doubleday, 2003.

*Jungmann, Joseph A., S.J. *The Mass of the Roman Rite: Its Origins and Development*. 2 vols. Translated by Francis A. Brunner. Notre Dame: Ave Maria Press, 2012.

Kreeft, Peter. *Letters to an Atheist: Wrestling with Faith*. Lanham, MD: Rowman & Littlefield, 2014.

Lewis, C. S. *God in the Dock: Essays on Theology and Ethics*. Grand Rapids, MI: Eerdmans, 1970.

*———. *Miracles: A Preliminary Study*. San Francisco: HarperOne, 2001.

Massa, Mark S., S.J. *The American Catholic Revolution: How the Sixties Changed the Church Forever*. New York: Oxford University Press, 2010.

———. *Anti-Catholicism in America: The Last Acceptable Prejudice*. New York: Crossroad, 2003.

Montessori, Maria. *The Mass Explained to Children*. Fort Collins, CO: Roman Catholic Books, 1932.

O'Connor, Flannery. *The Habit of Being: Letters of Flannery O'Connor*. Edited by Sally Fitzgerald. New York: Farrar, Straus and Giroux, 1979.

*O'Connor, James T. *The Hidden Manna: A Theology of the Eucharist*. San Francisco: Ignatius, 1988.

Ordway, Holly. *Not God's Type: An Atheist Academic Lays Down Her Arms*. San Francisco: Ignatius, 2014.

Otto, Rudolf. *The Idea of the Holy*. Translated by John W. Harvey. London: Oxford University Press, 1971.

Preaching the Mystery of Faith: The Sunday Homily. Washington, DC: United States Conference of Catholic Bishops, 2012.

Radcliffe, Timothy. *Why Go to Church? The Drama of the Eucharist*. London: Continuum, 2008.

*Ratzinger, Joseph Cardinal. *God Is Near Us: The Eucharist, the Heart of Life*. San Francisco: Ignatius, 2003.

———. *Introduction to Christianity*. Translated by J. R. Foster. San Francisco: Ignatius, 2004.

*———. *The Spirit of the Liturgy*. Translated by John Saward. San Francisco: Ignatius Press, 2000.

Rose, Devin. *The Protestant's Dilemma: How the Reformation's Shocking Consequences Point to the Truth of Catholicism*. San Diego: Catholic Answers, 2014.

Rosmini, Antonio. *Of the Five Wounds of the Holy Church*. Translated by Henry Parry Liddon. London: Rivingtons, 1883.

Scalia, Elizabeth. *Strange Gods: Unmasking the Idols in Everyday Life*. Notre Dame, IN: Ave Maria Press, 2013.

Von Speyr, Adrienne. *The Boundless God*. Translated by Helen M. Tomko. San Francisco: Ignatius, 2004.

Wiman, Christian. *My Bright Abyss: Meditation of a Modern Believer*. New York: Farrar, Straus and Giroux, 2013.

Wordsworth, William. *William Wordsworth*. Edited by Stephen Gill. Oxford: Oxford University Press, 1984.

Index

Paula Huston, a National Endowment for the Arts fellow, wrote literary fiction for more than twenty years before shifting her focus to spirituality. She taught writing and literature at Cal Poly, San Luis Obispo, and currently mentors graduate students in creative nonfiction for Seattle Pacific University's MFA in Creative Writing program.

Her first nonfiction project was *Signatures of Grace*, for which she served as coeditor and contributor; it earned a starred review from *Publishers Weekly*. Her book *The Holy Way*, which garnered another *PW* starred review, was a Catholic Press Association award-winner, a Catholic Book Club major selection, and a *ForeWord Magazine* bronze medalist for Book of the Year in Religion. Huston's other spiritual nonfiction includes *By Way of Grace*, *Forgiveness*, *Simplifying the Soul*, and *A Season of Mystery*. A Camaldolese Benedictine Oblate, Huston is married, has four children and four grandchildren, and lives on the central California coast.

AVE

AVE MARIA PRESS

Founded in 1865, Ave Maria Press,
a ministry of the Congregation of
Holy Cross, is a Catholic publishing
company that serves the spiritual and
formative needs of the Church and its
schools, institutions, and ministers;
Christian individuals and families; and
others seeking spiritual nourishment.

For a complete listing of titles from

Ave Maria Press

Sorin Books

Forest of Peace

Christian Classics

visit www.avemariapress.com

AVE MARIA PRESS
Notre Dame, IN
A Ministry of the United States Province of Holy Cross